60 Days of Math Practice

For 3rd Grade

Math Ninjas

Welcome to a journey where numbers come to life and equations dance with imagination! "Math Ninjas" is a captivating series designed to ignite the curiosity of budding mathematicians. With each turn of the page, children will embark on thrilling expeditions into the realm of numbers, shapes, and patterns.

Thank you for purchasing our Math Ninjas Book!,
we would like to offer you
A FREE BONUS Coloring Book!
Please scan the QR Code to receive it!

SCAN ME!

This Book Belongs to

_____

_____

1)
$$652 + 546$$

2)
$$660 + 495$$

3)
$$960 + 382$$

4)
$$740 + 882$$

5)
$$553 + 564$$

6)
$$446 + 147$$

7)
$$487 + 494$$

8)
$$400 + 335$$

9)
$$338 + 920$$

10)
$$208 + 458$$

11)
$$427 + 399$$

12)
$$317 + 799$$

13)
$$985 + 980$$

14)
$$690 + 639$$

15)
$$400 + 152$$

16)
$$594 + 391$$

17)
$$654 + 622$$

18)
$$869 + 407$$

19)
$$592 + 120$$

20)
$$352 + 391$$

21)
$$647 + 194$$

22)
$$147 + 980$$

23)
$$345 + 663$$

24)
$$442 + 641$$

25)
$$523 + 288$$

26)
$$442 + 233$$

27)
$$565 + 417$$

28)
$$901 + 184$$

29)
$$504 + 233$$

30)
$$565 + 278$$

31)
$$466 + 461$$

32)
$$979 + 760$$

33)
$$131 + 792$$

34)
$$452 + 797$$

35)
$$667 + 727$$

36)
$$154 + 528$$

37)
$$950 + 895$$

38)
$$746 + 208$$

39)
$$288 + 170$$

40)
$$253 + 276$$

1) 679 + 697

2) 391 + 910

3) 254 + 717

4) 737 + 247

5) 499 + 505

6) 795 + 244

7) 487 + 551

8) 175 + 514

9) 238 + 177

10) 293 + 449

11) 681 + 684

12) 536 + 356

13) 262 + 128

14) 429 + 651

15) 268 + 914

16) 934 + 573

17) 701 + 713

18) 807 + 359

19) 400 + 206

20) 632 + 524

21) 609 + 196

22) 310 + 332

23) 723 + 571

24) 517 + 596

25) 320 + 916

26) 325 + 990

27) 953 + 659

28) 964 + 400

29) 983 + 445

30) 427 + 121

31) 517 + 123

32) 445 + 884

33) 320 + 296

34) 196 + 548

35) 203 + 442

36) 164 + 428

37) 641 + 914

38) 902 + 294

39) 741 + 176

40) 858 + 565

1)
$$\begin{array}{r}\square \\ +\ 299 \\ \hline 1175 \end{array}$$

2)
$$\begin{array}{r}\square \\ +\ 101 \\ \hline 762 \end{array}$$

3)
$$\begin{array}{r}\square \\ +\ 937 \\ \hline 1694 \end{array}$$

4)
$$\begin{array}{r}\square \\ +\ 454 \\ \hline 1247 \end{array}$$

5)
$$\begin{array}{r}\square \\ +\ 747 \\ \hline 1250 \end{array}$$

6)
$$\begin{array}{r}\square \\ +\ 455 \\ \hline 1095 \end{array}$$

7)
$$\begin{array}{r}\square \\ +\ 749 \\ \hline 1533 \end{array}$$

8)
$$\begin{array}{r}\square \\ +\ 599 \\ \hline 889 \end{array}$$

9)
$$\begin{array}{r}\square \\ +\ 455 \\ \hline 1100 \end{array}$$

10)
$$\begin{array}{r}\square \\ +\ 540 \\ \hline 1011 \end{array}$$

11)
$$\begin{array}{r}\square \\ +\ 212 \\ \hline 414 \end{array}$$

12)
$$\begin{array}{r}\square \\ +\ 161 \\ \hline 527 \end{array}$$

13)
$$\begin{array}{r}\square \\ +\ 191 \\ \hline 861 \end{array}$$

14)
$$\begin{array}{r}\square \\ +\ 159 \\ \hline 969 \end{array}$$

15)
$$\begin{array}{r}\square \\ +\ 845 \\ \hline 962 \end{array}$$

16)
$$\begin{array}{r}\square \\ +\ 173 \\ \hline 610 \end{array}$$

17)
$$\begin{array}{r}\square \\ +\ 150 \\ \hline 508 \end{array}$$

18)
$$\begin{array}{r}\square \\ +\ 307 \\ \hline 800 \end{array}$$

19)
$$\begin{array}{r}\square \\ +\ 936 \\ \hline 1881 \end{array}$$

20)
$$\begin{array}{r}\square \\ +\ 197 \\ \hline 853 \end{array}$$

21)
$$\begin{array}{r}\square \\ +\ 367 \\ \hline 1000 \end{array}$$

22)
$$\begin{array}{r}\square \\ +\ 570 \\ \hline 1371 \end{array}$$

23)
$$\begin{array}{r}\square \\ +\ 179 \\ \hline 631 \end{array}$$

24)
$$\begin{array}{r}\square \\ +\ 961 \\ \hline 1480 \end{array}$$

25)
$$\begin{array}{r}\square \\ +\ 306 \\ \hline 1092 \end{array}$$

26)
$$\begin{array}{r}\square \\ +\ 374 \\ \hline 637 \end{array}$$

27)
$$\begin{array}{r}\square \\ +\ 879 \\ \hline 1284 \end{array}$$

28)
$$\begin{array}{r}\square \\ +\ 165 \\ \hline 1003 \end{array}$$

29)
$$\begin{array}{r}\square \\ +\ 855 \\ \hline 1150 \end{array}$$

30)
$$\begin{array}{r}\square \\ +\ 888 \\ \hline 1794 \end{array}$$

31)
$$\begin{array}{r}\square \\ +\ 735 \\ \hline 940 \end{array}$$

32)
$$\begin{array}{r}\square \\ +\ 916 \\ \hline 1867 \end{array}$$

33)
$$\begin{array}{r}\square \\ +\ 520 \\ \hline 1001 \end{array}$$

34)
$$\begin{array}{r}\square \\ +\ 373 \\ \hline 561 \end{array}$$

35)
$$\begin{array}{r}\square \\ +\ 339 \\ \hline 1052 \end{array}$$

36)
$$\begin{array}{r}\square \\ +\ 622 \\ \hline 1190 \end{array}$$

37)
$$\begin{array}{r}\square \\ +\ 576 \\ \hline 1091 \end{array}$$

38)
$$\begin{array}{r}\square \\ +\ 881 \\ \hline 1744 \end{array}$$

39)
$$\begin{array}{r}\square \\ +\ 233 \\ \hline 816 \end{array}$$

40)
$$\begin{array}{r}\square \\ +\ 172 \\ \hline 1133 \end{array}$$

1)
```
  [    ]
+  775
 1337
```

2)
```
  [    ]
+  569
  927
```

3)
```
  [    ]
+  887
 1877
```

4)
```
  [    ]
+  724
 1065
```

5)
```
  [    ]
+  931
 1455
```

6)
```
  [    ]
+  561
 1108
```

7)
```
  [    ]
+  362
  547
```

8)
```
  [    ]
+  640
 1046
```

9)
```
  [    ]
+  473
 1472
```

10)
```
  [    ]
+  514
  850
```

11)
```
  [    ]
+  223
  727
```

12)
```
  [    ]
+  481
 1354
```

13)
```
  [    ]
+  565
 1281
```

14)
```
  [    ]
+  963
 1548
```

15)
```
  [    ]
+  593
 1569
```

16)
```
  [    ]
+  982
 1586
```

17)
```
  [    ]
+  863
 1460
```

18)
```
  [    ]
+  612
 1155
```

19)
```
  [    ]
+  824
 1409
```

20)
```
  [    ]
+  305
  859
```

21)
```
  [    ]
+  528
  798
```

22)
```
  [    ]
+  996
 1525
```

23)
```
  [    ]
+  137
  478
```

24)
```
  [    ]
+  824
 1570
```

25)
```
  [    ]
+  946
 1613
```

26)
```
  [    ]
+  481
 1203
```

27)
```
  [    ]
+  289
 1103
```

28)
```
  [    ]
+  313
  877
```

29)
```
  [    ]
+  764
 1051
```

30)
```
  [    ]
+  612
 1511
```

31)
```
  [    ]
+  724
 1171
```

32)
```
  [    ]
+  199
  771
```

33)
```
  [    ]
+  850
 1120
```

34)
```
  [    ]
+  126
 1118
```

35)
```
  [    ]
+  190
  599
```

36)
```
  [    ]
+  997
 1347
```

37)
```
  [    ]
+  977
 1107
```

38)
```
  [    ]
+  113
  356
```

39)
```
  [    ]
+  239
 1154
```

40)
```
  [    ]
+  324
  749
```

1) 862 + ____ = 997

2) 694 + ____ = 1341

3) 681 + ____ = 1041

4) 321 + ____ = 1130

5) 114 + ____ = 621

6) 442 + ____ = 1134

7) 808 + ____ = 1644

8) 241 + ____ = 707

9) 780 + ____ = 1069

10) 680 + ____ = 1264

11) 668 + ____ = 1169

12) 179 + ____ = 955

13) 909 + ____ = 1537

14) 890 + ____ = 1241

15) 989 + ____ = 1884

16) 128 + ____ = 744

17) 864 + ____ = 1343

18) 570 + ____ = 1037

19) 527 + ____ = 1380

20) 171 + ____ = 831

21) 670 + ____ = 847

22) 817 + ____ = 1503

23) 348 + ____ = 1167

24) 945 + ____ = 1867

25) 462 + ____ = 803

26) 223 + ____ = 528

27) 902 + ____ = 1750

28) 718 + ____ = 1623

29) 491 + ____ = 797

30) 108 + ____ = 474

31) 401 + ____ = 1045

32) 553 + ____ = 1042

33) 679 + ____ = 1137

34) 905 + ____ = 1518

35) 624 + ____ = 1143

36) 344 + ____ = 1140

37) 190 + ____ = 376

38) 403 + ____ = 933

39) 902 + ____ = 1823

40) 845 + ____ = 1766

1)
$$691 + 363$$

2)
$$939 + 656$$

3)
$$565 + 435$$

4)
$$165 + 609$$

5)
$$171 + 457$$

6)
$$298 + 936$$

7)
$$518 + 311$$

8)
$$976 + 841$$

9)
$$843 + 547$$

10)
$$505 + 689$$

11)
$$952 + 690$$

12)
$$927 + 485$$

13)
$$630 + 934$$

14)
$$213 + 804$$

15)
$$319 + 804$$

16)
$$197 + 890$$

17)
$$596 + 103$$

18)
$$570 + 220$$

19)
$$251 + 873$$

20)
$$631 + 755$$

21)
$$795 + 507$$

22)
$$876 + 846$$

23)
$$271 + 792$$

24)
$$546 + 611$$

25)
$$925 + 168$$

26)
$$864 + 604$$

27)
$$393 + 249$$

28)
$$314 + 379$$

29)
$$239 + 753$$

30)
$$956 + 716$$

31)
$$487 + 688$$

32)
$$828 + 891$$

33)
$$659 + 565$$

34)
$$640 + 247$$

35)
$$893 + 745$$

36)
$$770 + 495$$

37)
$$287 + 284$$

38)
$$676 + 329$$

39)
$$473 + 198$$

40)
$$316 + 395$$

1)
$$288 + \boxed{} = 781$$

2)
$$729 + \boxed{} = 896$$

3)
$$720 + \boxed{} = 1537$$

4)
$$532 + \boxed{} = 1067$$

5)
$$274 + \boxed{} = 1234$$

6)
$$719 + \boxed{} = 1246$$

7)
$$296 + \boxed{} = 451$$

8)
$$123 + \boxed{} = 942$$

9)
$$965 + \boxed{} = 1320$$

10)
$$181 + \boxed{} = 821$$

11)
$$423 + \boxed{} = 803$$

12)
$$416 + \boxed{} = 1356$$

13)
$$416 + \boxed{} = 951$$

14)
$$804 + \boxed{} = 1658$$

15)
$$208 + \boxed{} = 330$$

16)
$$376 + \boxed{} = 1205$$

17)
$$664 + \boxed{} = 829$$

18)
$$178 + \boxed{} = 1153$$

19)
$$750 + \boxed{} = 1310$$

20)
$$604 + \boxed{} = 1600$$

21)
$$589 + \boxed{} = 902$$

22)
$$513 + \boxed{} = 1322$$

23)
$$256 + \boxed{} = 356$$

24)
$$597 + \boxed{} = 1218$$

25)
$$252 + \boxed{} = 455$$

26)
$$415 + \boxed{} = 1362$$

27)
$$189 + \boxed{} = 748$$

28)
$$337 + \boxed{} = 1312$$

29)
$$748 + \boxed{} = 1181$$

30)
$$130 + \boxed{} = 337$$

31)
$$511 + \boxed{} = 1224$$

32)
$$240 + \boxed{} = 570$$

33)
$$439 + \boxed{} = 1435$$

34)
$$303 + \boxed{} = 428$$

35)
$$276 + \boxed{} = 496$$

36)
$$950 + \boxed{} = 1858$$

37)
$$911 + \boxed{} = 1080$$

38)
$$685 + \boxed{} = 1300$$

39)
$$846 + \boxed{} = 1159$$

40)
$$650 + \boxed{} = 1507$$

1) 397 + _____ = 1110

2) 535 + _____ = 1300

3) 488 + _____ = 1438

4) 276 + _____ = 472

5) 787 + _____ = 973

6) 378 + _____ = 735

7) 749 + _____ = 1364

8) 783 + _____ = 1385

9) 294 + _____ = 674

10) 782 + _____ = 1277

11) 321 + _____ = 583

12) 330 + _____ = 812

13) 706 + _____ = 1163

14) 727 + _____ = 1181

15) 900 + _____ = 1133

16) 907 + _____ = 1008

17) 609 + _____ = 885

18) 555 + _____ = 722

19) 623 + _____ = 1584

20) 333 + _____ = 1245

21) 347 + _____ = 1007

22) 534 + _____ = 1405

23) 420 + _____ = 1402

24) 157 + _____ = 821

25) 526 + _____ = 1490

26) 572 + _____ = 962

27) 274 + _____ = 602

28) 954 + _____ = 1816

29) 186 + _____ = 754

30) 489 + _____ = 1172

31) 723 + _____ = 1596

32) 307 + _____ = 617

33) 205 + _____ = 613

34) 577 + _____ = 908

35) 533 + _____ = 1289

36) 559 + _____ = 710

37) 567 + _____ = 1131

38) 202 + _____ = 763

39) 870 + _____ = 1294

40) 318 + _____ = 1248

1) 876
  − 253

2) 216
  − 137

3) 730
  − 230

4) 637
  − 151

5) 141
  − 136

6) 791
  − 791

7) 924
  − 455

8) 789
  − 231

9) 743
  − 469

10) 796
  − 136

11) 930
  − 475

12) 709
  − 253

13) 936
  − 649

14) 523
  − 382

15) 983
  − 333

16) 866
  − 458

17) 805
  − 407

18) 846
  − 324

19) 786
  − 785

20) 781
  − 698

21) 590
  − 101

22) 322
  − 271

23) 734
  − 177

24) 899
  − 125

25) 574
  − 173

26) 938
  − 744

27) 431
  − 398

28) 606
  − 317

29) 368
  − 283

30) 634
  − 570

31) 582
  − 114

32) 879
  − 168

33) 749
  − 595

34) 843
  − 377

35) 319
  − 262

36) 716
  − 325

37) 674
  − 546

38) 524
  − 166

39) 883
  − 726

40) 652
  − 365

1) 438
  − 298

2) 476
  − 449

3) 727
  − 268

4) 896
  − 448

5) 877
  − 842

6) 893
  − 660

7) 459
  − 105

8) 892
  − 226

9) 283
  − 131

10) 287
  − 192

11) 912
  − 244

12) 939
  − 414

13) 555
  − 271

14) 580
  − 107

15) 717
  − 430

16) 403
  − 195

17) 501
  − 102

18) 380
  − 225

19) 680
  − 594

20) 345
  − 281

21) 946
  − 329

22) 686
  − 444

23) 334
  − 233

24) 722
  − 380

25) 964
  − 950

26) 869
  − 170

27) 440
  − 353

28) 845
  − 715

29) 566
  − 134

30) 461
  − 401

31) 888
  − 142

32) 719
  − 178

33) 451
  − 118

34) 508
  − 375

35) 626
  − 132

36) 435
  − 333

37) 601
  − 530

38) 519
  − 137

39) 812
  − 728

40) 464
  − 108

1)
```
  ☐
- 472
  438
```

2)
```
  ☐
- 105
  118
```

3)
```
  ☐
- 676
   57
```

4)
```
  ☐
- 279
  116
```

5)
```
  ☐
- 773
  127
```

6)
```
  ☐
- 535
   45
```

7)
```
  ☐
- 352
   45
```

8)
```
  ☐
- 171
  718
```

9)
```
  ☐
- 541
  148
```

10)
```
  ☐
- 497
  365
```

11)
```
  ☐
- 213
   93
```

12)
```
  ☐
- 539
  205
```

13)
```
  ☐
- 656
   57
```

14)
```
  ☐
- 590
  214
```

15)
```
  ☐
- 271
  504
```

16)
```
  ☐
- 685
  200
```

17)
```
  ☐
- 556
   90
```

18)
```
  ☐
- 617
   83
```

19)
```
  ☐
- 142
  175
```

20)
```
  ☐
- 540
  358
```

21)
```
  ☐
- 738
  211
```

22)
```
  ☐
- 502
  274
```

23)
```
  ☐
- 524
  379
```

24)
```
  ☐
- 608
  296
```

25)
```
  ☐
- 484
   92
```

26)
```
  ☐
- 432
  286
```

27)
```
  ☐
- 211
  284
```

28)
```
  ☐
- 259
  654
```

29)
```
  ☐
- 218
  396
```

30)
```
  ☐
- 328
  593
```

31)
```
  ☐
- 706
  102
```

32)
```
  ☐
- 671
  251
```

33)
```
  ☐
- 161
  563
```

34)
```
  ☐
- 389
  209
```

35)
```
  ☐
- 166
  690
```

36)
```
  ☐
- 727
   81
```

37)
```
  ☐
- 317
  136
```

38)
```
  ☐
- 299
  464
```

39)
```
  ☐
- 483
  484
```

40)
```
  ☐
- 171
   64
```

1)   844
  − 506
  [____]

2)   428
  − 218
  [____]

3)   901
  − 499
  [____]

4)   730
  − 290
  [____]

5)   756
  − 570
  [____]

6)   457
  − 213
  [____]

7)   843
  − 328
  [____]

8)   847
  − 757
  [____]

9)   852
  − 524
  [____]

10)   917
  − 824
  [____]

11)   681
  − 330
  [____]

12)   572
  − 279
  [____]

13)   932
  − 303
  [____]

14)   747
  − 326
  [____]

15)   991
  − 595
  [____]

16)   402
  − 292
  [____]

17)   950
  − 609
  [____]

18)   240
  − 118
  [____]

19)   651
  − 532
  [____]

20)   719
  − 502
  [____]

21)   628
  − 273
  [____]

22)   956
  − 700
  [____]

23)   774
  − 741
  [____]

24)   585
  − 283
  [____]

25)   380
  − 196
  [____]

26)   801
  − 363
  [____]

27)   339
  − 179
  [____]

28)   583
  − 520
  [____]

29)   881
  − 214
  [____]

30)   987
  − 114
  [____]

31)   608
  − 520
  [____]

32)   785
  − 692
  [____]

33)   472
  − 220
  [____]

34)   388
  − 131
  [____]

35)   780
  − 534
  [____]

36)   697
  − 281
  [____]

37)   666
  − 634
  [____]

38)   581
  − 302
  [____]

39)   905
  − 643
  [____]

40)   731
  − 321
  [____]

1)
$$\begin{array}{r} \boxed{} \\ -\ 513 \\ \hline 25 \end{array}$$

2)
$$\begin{array}{r} \boxed{} \\ -\ 379 \\ \hline 160 \end{array}$$

3)
$$\begin{array}{r} \boxed{} \\ -\ 203 \\ \hline 462 \end{array}$$

4)
$$\begin{array}{r} \boxed{} \\ -\ 761 \\ \hline 37 \end{array}$$

5)
$$\begin{array}{r} \boxed{} \\ -\ 133 \\ \hline 162 \end{array}$$

6)
$$\begin{array}{r} \boxed{} \\ -\ 375 \\ \hline 142 \end{array}$$

7)
$$\begin{array}{r} \boxed{} \\ -\ 327 \\ \hline 443 \end{array}$$

8)
$$\begin{array}{r} \boxed{} \\ -\ 600 \\ \hline 375 \end{array}$$

9)
$$\begin{array}{r} \boxed{} \\ -\ 369 \\ \hline 394 \end{array}$$

10)
$$\begin{array}{r} \boxed{} \\ -\ 211 \\ \hline 181 \end{array}$$

11)
$$\begin{array}{r} \boxed{} \\ -\ 338 \\ \hline 502 \end{array}$$

12)
$$\begin{array}{r} \boxed{} \\ -\ 510 \\ \hline 268 \end{array}$$

13)
$$\begin{array}{r} \boxed{} \\ -\ 656 \\ \hline 250 \end{array}$$

14)
$$\begin{array}{r} \boxed{} \\ -\ 366 \\ \hline 213 \end{array}$$

15)
$$\begin{array}{r} \boxed{} \\ -\ 869 \\ \hline 108 \end{array}$$

16)
$$\begin{array}{r} \boxed{} \\ -\ 537 \\ \hline 81 \end{array}$$

17)
$$\begin{array}{r} \boxed{} \\ -\ 242 \\ \hline 529 \end{array}$$

18)
$$\begin{array}{r} \boxed{} \\ -\ 242 \\ \hline 645 \end{array}$$

19)
$$\begin{array}{r} \boxed{} \\ -\ 134 \\ \hline 198 \end{array}$$

20)
$$\begin{array}{r} \boxed{} \\ -\ 447 \\ \hline 159 \end{array}$$

21)
$$\begin{array}{r} \boxed{} \\ -\ 643 \\ \hline 297 \end{array}$$

22)
$$\begin{array}{r} \boxed{} \\ -\ 264 \\ \hline 76 \end{array}$$

23)
$$\begin{array}{r} \boxed{} \\ -\ 161 \\ \hline 699 \end{array}$$

24)
$$\begin{array}{r} \boxed{} \\ -\ 333 \\ \hline 578 \end{array}$$

25)
$$\begin{array}{r} \boxed{} \\ -\ 585 \\ \hline 151 \end{array}$$

26)
$$\begin{array}{r} \boxed{} \\ -\ 104 \\ \hline 822 \end{array}$$

27)
$$\begin{array}{r} \boxed{} \\ -\ 416 \\ \hline 174 \end{array}$$

28)
$$\begin{array}{r} \boxed{} \\ -\ 124 \\ \hline 474 \end{array}$$

29)
$$\begin{array}{r} \boxed{} \\ -\ 236 \\ \hline 636 \end{array}$$

30)
$$\begin{array}{r} \boxed{} \\ -\ 894 \\ \hline 26 \end{array}$$

31)
$$\begin{array}{r} \boxed{} \\ -\ 230 \\ \hline 129 \end{array}$$

32)
$$\begin{array}{r} \boxed{} \\ -\ 634 \\ \hline 93 \end{array}$$

33)
$$\begin{array}{r} \boxed{} \\ -\ 113 \\ \hline 446 \end{array}$$

34)
$$\begin{array}{r} \boxed{} \\ -\ 921 \\ \hline 74 \end{array}$$

35)
$$\begin{array}{r} \boxed{} \\ -\ 417 \\ \hline 130 \end{array}$$

36)
$$\begin{array}{r} \boxed{} \\ -\ 669 \\ \hline 53 \end{array}$$

37)
$$\begin{array}{r} \boxed{} \\ -\ 354 \\ \hline 511 \end{array}$$

38)
$$\begin{array}{r} \boxed{} \\ -\ 323 \\ \hline 338 \end{array}$$

39)
$$\begin{array}{r} \boxed{} \\ -\ 249 \\ \hline 594 \end{array}$$

40)
$$\begin{array}{r} \boxed{} \\ -\ 392 \\ \hline 469 \end{array}$$

1)
$$701 - \boxed{} = 118$$

2)
$$992 - \boxed{} = 367$$

3)
$$621 - \boxed{} = 21$$

4)
$$985 - \boxed{} = 456$$

5)
$$372 - \boxed{} = 84$$

6)
$$771 - \boxed{} = 465$$

7)
$$892 - \boxed{} = 550$$

8)
$$643 - \boxed{} = 479$$

9)
$$941 - \boxed{} = 272$$

10)
$$448 - \boxed{} = 291$$

11)
$$846 - \boxed{} = 552$$

12)
$$656 - \boxed{} = 254$$

13)
$$418 - \boxed{} = 53$$

14)
$$662 - \boxed{} = 209$$

15)
$$842 - \boxed{} = 312$$

16)
$$964 - \boxed{} = 770$$

17)
$$588 - \boxed{} = 179$$

18)
$$953 - \boxed{} = 347$$

19)
$$354 - \boxed{} = 19$$

20)
$$785 - \boxed{} = 220$$

21)
$$324 - \boxed{} = 32$$

22)
$$978 - \boxed{} = 213$$

23)
$$382 - \boxed{} = 73$$

24)
$$698 - \boxed{} = 169$$

25)
$$712 - \boxed{} = 399$$

26)
$$927 - \boxed{} = 254$$

27)
$$458 - \boxed{} = 91$$

28)
$$957 - \boxed{} = 617$$

29)
$$984 - \boxed{} = 44$$

30)
$$858 - \boxed{} = 756$$

31)
$$560 - \boxed{} = 199$$

32)
$$820 - \boxed{} = 372$$

33)
$$862 - \boxed{} = 337$$

34)
$$870 - \boxed{} = 505$$

35)
$$397 - \boxed{} = 242$$

36)
$$807 - \boxed{} = 192$$

37)
$$845 - \boxed{} = 8$$

38)
$$969 - \boxed{} = 353$$

39)
$$925 - \boxed{} = 504$$

40)
$$867 - \boxed{} = 617$$

1)
$$\begin{array}{r} 599 \\ - \\ \hline 76 \end{array}$$

2)
$$\begin{array}{r} 802 \\ - \\ \hline 354 \end{array}$$

3)
$$\begin{array}{r} 420 \\ - \\ \hline 4 \end{array}$$

4)
$$\begin{array}{r} 499 \\ - \\ \hline 286 \end{array}$$

5)
$$\begin{array}{r} 622 \\ - \\ \hline 444 \end{array}$$

6)
$$\begin{array}{r} 227 \\ - \\ \hline 120 \end{array}$$

7)
$$\begin{array}{r} 830 \\ - \\ \hline 730 \end{array}$$

8)
$$\begin{array}{r} 966 \\ - \\ \hline 343 \end{array}$$

9)
$$\begin{array}{r} 806 \\ - \\ \hline 133 \end{array}$$

10)
$$\begin{array}{r} 795 \\ - \\ \hline 371 \end{array}$$

11)
$$\begin{array}{r} 869 \\ - \\ \hline 289 \end{array}$$

12)
$$\begin{array}{r} 731 \\ - \\ \hline 493 \end{array}$$

13)
$$\begin{array}{r} 424 \\ - \\ \hline 115 \end{array}$$

14)
$$\begin{array}{r} 715 \\ - \\ \hline 43 \end{array}$$

15)
$$\begin{array}{r} 592 \\ - \\ \hline 78 \end{array}$$

16)
$$\begin{array}{r} 990 \\ - \\ \hline 663 \end{array}$$

17)
$$\begin{array}{r} 964 \\ - \\ \hline 110 \end{array}$$

18)
$$\begin{array}{r} 787 \\ - \\ \hline 135 \end{array}$$

19)
$$\begin{array}{r} 251 \\ - \\ \hline 1 \end{array}$$

20)
$$\begin{array}{r} 620 \\ - \\ \hline 233 \end{array}$$

21)
$$\begin{array}{r} 836 \\ - \\ \hline 584 \end{array}$$

22)
$$\begin{array}{r} 752 \\ - \\ \hline 336 \end{array}$$

23)
$$\begin{array}{r} 852 \\ - \\ \hline 704 \end{array}$$

24)
$$\begin{array}{r} 735 \\ - \\ \hline 533 \end{array}$$

25)
$$\begin{array}{r} 785 \\ - \\ \hline 553 \end{array}$$

26)
$$\begin{array}{r} 184 \\ - \\ \hline 54 \end{array}$$

27)
$$\begin{array}{r} 813 \\ - \\ \hline 146 \end{array}$$

28)
$$\begin{array}{r} 201 \\ - \\ \hline 17 \end{array}$$

29)
$$\begin{array}{r} 786 \\ - \\ \hline 295 \end{array}$$

30)
$$\begin{array}{r} 511 \\ - \\ \hline 395 \end{array}$$

31)
$$\begin{array}{r} 680 \\ - \\ \hline 534 \end{array}$$

32)
$$\begin{array}{r} 425 \\ - \\ \hline 260 \end{array}$$

33)
$$\begin{array}{r} 998 \\ - \\ \hline 572 \end{array}$$

34)
$$\begin{array}{r} 915 \\ - \\ \hline 566 \end{array}$$

35)
$$\begin{array}{r} 920 \\ - \\ \hline 587 \end{array}$$

36)
$$\begin{array}{r} 969 \\ - \\ \hline 525 \end{array}$$

37)
$$\begin{array}{r} 681 \\ - \\ \hline 307 \end{array}$$

38)
$$\begin{array}{r} 465 \\ - \\ \hline 98 \end{array}$$

39)
$$\begin{array}{r} 942 \\ - \\ \hline 38 \end{array}$$

40)
$$\begin{array}{r} 684 \\ - \\ \hline 400 \end{array}$$

1) 954
  − 825

2) 264
  − 106

3) 391
  − 326

4) 218
  − 127

5) 784
  − 245

6) 932
  − 563

7) 226
  − 185

8) 207
  − 150

9) 350
  − 143

10) 449
  − 391

11) 851
  − 422

12) 626
  − 355

13) 992
  − 328

14) 321
  − 177

15) 661
  − 624

16) 325
  − 143

17) 804
  − 380

18) 661
  − 149

19) 894
  − 416

20) 712
  − 603

21) 696
  − 529

22) 609
  − 538

23) 904
  − 463

24) 785
  − 538

25) 661
  − 228

26) 948
  − 884

27) 940
  − 554

28) 751
  − 196

29) 695
  − 307

30) 673
  − 314

31) 865
  − 439

32) 333
  − 244

33) 837
  − 549

34) 948
  − 174

35) 664
  − 627

36) 321
  − 174

37) 910
  − 785

38) 943
  − 725

39) 746
  − 439

40) 853
  − 390

1) $\begin{array}{r} 7 \\ \times\ 4 \\ \hline \end{array}$

2) $\begin{array}{r} 8 \\ \times\ 7 \\ \hline \end{array}$

3) $\begin{array}{r} 9 \\ \times\ 3 \\ \hline \end{array}$

4) $\begin{array}{r} 5 \\ \times\ 9 \\ \hline \end{array}$

5) $\begin{array}{r} 4 \\ \times\ 5 \\ \hline \end{array}$

6) $\begin{array}{r} 1 \\ \times\ 7 \\ \hline \end{array}$

7) $\begin{array}{r} 1 \\ \times\ 1 \\ \hline \end{array}$

8) $\begin{array}{r} 6 \\ \times\ 6 \\ \hline \end{array}$

9) $\begin{array}{r} 2 \\ \times\ 1 \\ \hline \end{array}$

10) $\begin{array}{r} 8 \\ \times\ 2 \\ \hline \end{array}$

11) $\begin{array}{r} 7 \\ \times\ 7 \\ \hline \end{array}$

12) $\begin{array}{r} 3 \\ \times\ 6 \\ \hline \end{array}$

13) $\begin{array}{r} 3 \\ \times\ 1 \\ \hline \end{array}$

14) $\begin{array}{r} 3 \\ \times\ 7 \\ \hline \end{array}$

15) $\begin{array}{r} 9 \\ \times\ 9 \\ \hline \end{array}$

16) $\begin{array}{r} 4 \\ \times\ 1 \\ \hline \end{array}$

17) $\begin{array}{r} 5 \\ \times\ 4 \\ \hline \end{array}$

18) $\begin{array}{r} 5 \\ \times\ 1 \\ \hline \end{array}$

19) $\begin{array}{r} 8 \\ \times\ 3 \\ \hline \end{array}$

20) $\begin{array}{r} 5 \\ \times\ 1 \\ \hline \end{array}$

21) $\begin{array}{r} 3 \\ \times\ 2 \\ \hline \end{array}$

22) $\begin{array}{r} 4 \\ \times\ 4 \\ \hline \end{array}$

23) $\begin{array}{r} 5 \\ \times\ 6 \\ \hline \end{array}$

24) $\begin{array}{r} 8 \\ \times\ 5 \\ \hline \end{array}$

25) $\begin{array}{r} 9 \\ \times\ 3 \\ \hline \end{array}$

26) $\begin{array}{r} 8 \\ \times\ 1 \\ \hline \end{array}$

27) $\begin{array}{r} 2 \\ \times\ 2 \\ \hline \end{array}$

28) $\begin{array}{r} 5 \\ \times\ 6 \\ \hline \end{array}$

29) $\begin{array}{r} 1 \\ \times\ 9 \\ \hline \end{array}$

30) $\begin{array}{r} 7 \\ \times\ 1 \\ \hline \end{array}$

31) $\begin{array}{r} 2 \\ \times\ 3 \\ \hline \end{array}$

32) $\begin{array}{r} 9 \\ \times\ 3 \\ \hline \end{array}$

33) $\begin{array}{r} 3 \\ \times\ 8 \\ \hline \end{array}$

34) $\begin{array}{r} 9 \\ \times\ 2 \\ \hline \end{array}$

35) $\begin{array}{r} 7 \\ \times\ 1 \\ \hline \end{array}$

36) $\begin{array}{r} 1 \\ \times\ 8 \\ \hline \end{array}$

37) $\begin{array}{r} 7 \\ \times\ 9 \\ \hline \end{array}$

38) $\begin{array}{r} 6 \\ \times\ 6 \\ \hline \end{array}$

39) $\begin{array}{r} 1 \\ \times\ 8 \\ \hline \end{array}$

40) $\begin{array}{r} 3 \\ \times\ 7 \\ \hline \end{array}$

1)   3
× 3

2)   4
× 3

3)   8
× 8

4)   9
× 9

5)   9
× 7

6)   7
× 3

7)   2
× 3

8)   6
× 5

9)   6
× 3

10)   4
× 1

11)   1
× 5

12)   5
× 5

13)   4
× 3

14)   2
× 9

15)   5
× 9

16)   4
× 8

17)   6
× 7

18)   3
× 4

19)   5
× 1

20)   4
× 1

21)   1
× 8

22)   6
× 9

23)   2
× 8

24)   9
× 4

25)   7
× 8

26)   7
× 1

27)   5
× 6

28)   7
× 5

29)   4
× 1

30)   2
× 4

31)   6
× 4

32)   5
× 2

33)   8
× 5

34)   5
× 2

35)   6
× 8

36)   2
× 7

37)   9
× 9

38)   1
× 3

39)   8
× 5

40)   8
× 3

1) $\begin{array}{r} 7 \\ \times\ 3 \\ \hline \end{array}$

2) $\begin{array}{r} 5 \\ \times\ 1 \\ \hline \end{array}$

3) $\begin{array}{r} 5 \\ \times\ 4 \\ \hline \end{array}$

4) $\begin{array}{r} 1 \\ \times\ 5 \\ \hline \end{array}$

5) $\begin{array}{r} 4 \\ \times\ 2 \\ \hline \end{array}$

6) $\begin{array}{r} 7 \\ \times\ 3 \\ \hline \end{array}$

7) $\begin{array}{r} 2 \\ \times\ 6 \\ \hline \end{array}$

8) $\begin{array}{r} 6 \\ \times\ 5 \\ \hline \end{array}$

9) $\begin{array}{r} 5 \\ \times\ 8 \\ \hline \end{array}$

10) $\begin{array}{r} 7 \\ \times\ 9 \\ \hline \end{array}$

11) $\begin{array}{r} 1 \\ \times\ 2 \\ \hline \end{array}$

12) $\begin{array}{r} 6 \\ \times\ 5 \\ \hline \end{array}$

13) $\begin{array}{r} 4 \\ \times\ 6 \\ \hline \end{array}$

14) $\begin{array}{r} 2 \\ \times\ 4 \\ \hline \end{array}$

15) $\begin{array}{r} 7 \\ \times\ 7 \\ \hline \end{array}$

16) $\begin{array}{r} 4 \\ \times\ 9 \\ \hline \end{array}$

17) $\begin{array}{r} 7 \\ \times\ 3 \\ \hline \end{array}$

18) $\begin{array}{r} 3 \\ \times\ 5 \\ \hline \end{array}$

19) $\begin{array}{r} 7 \\ \times\ 1 \\ \hline \end{array}$

20) $\begin{array}{r} 9 \\ \times\ 4 \\ \hline \end{array}$

21) $\begin{array}{r} 9 \\ \times\ 5 \\ \hline \end{array}$

22) $\begin{array}{r} 8 \\ \times\ 6 \\ \hline \end{array}$

23) $\begin{array}{r} 2 \\ \times\ 6 \\ \hline \end{array}$

24) $\begin{array}{r} 8 \\ \times\ 4 \\ \hline \end{array}$

25) $\begin{array}{r} 1 \\ \times\ 2 \\ \hline \end{array}$

26) $\begin{array}{r} 1 \\ \times\ 5 \\ \hline \end{array}$

27) $\begin{array}{r} 1 \\ \times\ 3 \\ \hline \end{array}$

28) $\begin{array}{r} 6 \\ \times\ 4 \\ \hline \end{array}$

29) $\begin{array}{r} 7 \\ \times\ 5 \\ \hline \end{array}$

30) $\begin{array}{r} 6 \\ \times\ 6 \\ \hline \end{array}$

31) $\begin{array}{r} 7 \\ \times\ 8 \\ \hline \end{array}$

32) $\begin{array}{r} 4 \\ \times\ 2 \\ \hline \end{array}$

33) $\begin{array}{r} 7 \\ \times\ 3 \\ \hline \end{array}$

34) $\begin{array}{r} 4 \\ \times\ 3 \\ \hline \end{array}$

35) $\begin{array}{r} 6 \\ \times\ 8 \\ \hline \end{array}$

36) $\begin{array}{r} 6 \\ \times\ 6 \\ \hline \end{array}$

37) $\begin{array}{r} 6 \\ \times\ 5 \\ \hline \end{array}$

38) $\begin{array}{r} 5 \\ \times\ 4 \\ \hline \end{array}$

39) $\begin{array}{r} 9 \\ \times\ 4 \\ \hline \end{array}$

40) $\begin{array}{r} 6 \\ \times\ 6 \\ \hline \end{array}$

1) $\begin{array}{r} 5 \\ \times\ 7 \\ \hline \end{array}$

2) $\begin{array}{r} 8 \\ \times\ 3 \\ \hline \end{array}$

3) $\begin{array}{r} 3 \\ \times\ 3 \\ \hline \end{array}$

4) $\begin{array}{r} 6 \\ \times\ 1 \\ \hline \end{array}$

5) $\begin{array}{r} 1 \\ \times\ 3 \\ \hline \end{array}$

6) $\begin{array}{r} 2 \\ \times\ 5 \\ \hline \end{array}$

7) $\begin{array}{r} 6 \\ \times\ 3 \\ \hline \end{array}$

8) $\begin{array}{r} 6 \\ \times\ 4 \\ \hline \end{array}$

9) $\begin{array}{r} 3 \\ \times\ 1 \\ \hline \end{array}$

10) $\begin{array}{r} 1 \\ \times\ 4 \\ \hline \end{array}$

11) $\begin{array}{r} 8 \\ \times\ 3 \\ \hline \end{array}$

12) $\begin{array}{r} 2 \\ \times\ 5 \\ \hline \end{array}$

13) $\begin{array}{r} 4 \\ \times\ 5 \\ \hline \end{array}$

14) $\begin{array}{r} 3 \\ \times\ 3 \\ \hline \end{array}$

15) $\begin{array}{r} 1 \\ \times\ 5 \\ \hline \end{array}$

16) $\begin{array}{r} 4 \\ \times\ 4 \\ \hline \end{array}$

17) $\begin{array}{r} 3 \\ \times\ 9 \\ \hline \end{array}$

18) $\begin{array}{r} 7 \\ \times\ 9 \\ \hline \end{array}$

19) $\begin{array}{r} 5 \\ \times\ 6 \\ \hline \end{array}$

20) $\begin{array}{r} 5 \\ \times\ 3 \\ \hline \end{array}$

21) $\begin{array}{r} 5 \\ \times\ 9 \\ \hline \end{array}$

22) $\begin{array}{r} 9 \\ \times\ 5 \\ \hline \end{array}$

23) $\begin{array}{r} 3 \\ \times\ 4 \\ \hline \end{array}$

24) $\begin{array}{r} 1 \\ \times\ 4 \\ \hline \end{array}$

25) $\begin{array}{r} 5 \\ \times\ 2 \\ \hline \end{array}$

26) $\begin{array}{r} 2 \\ \times\ 2 \\ \hline \end{array}$

27) $\begin{array}{r} 2 \\ \times\ 9 \\ \hline \end{array}$

28) $\begin{array}{r} 2 \\ \times\ 4 \\ \hline \end{array}$

29) $\begin{array}{r} 1 \\ \times\ 7 \\ \hline \end{array}$

30) $\begin{array}{r} 3 \\ \times\ 3 \\ \hline \end{array}$

31) $\begin{array}{r} 8 \\ \times\ 8 \\ \hline \end{array}$

32) $\begin{array}{r} 3 \\ \times\ 4 \\ \hline \end{array}$

33) $\begin{array}{r} 7 \\ \times\ 3 \\ \hline \end{array}$

34) $\begin{array}{r} 2 \\ \times\ 4 \\ \hline \end{array}$

35) $\begin{array}{r} 4 \\ \times\ 6 \\ \hline \end{array}$

36) $\begin{array}{r} 1 \\ \times\ 2 \\ \hline \end{array}$

37) $\begin{array}{r} 7 \\ \times\ 9 \\ \hline \end{array}$

38) $\begin{array}{r} 1 \\ \times\ 5 \\ \hline \end{array}$

39) $\begin{array}{r} 6 \\ \times\ 1 \\ \hline \end{array}$

40) $\begin{array}{r} 1 \\ \times\ 8 \\ \hline \end{array}$

1) $\begin{array}{r} \square \\ \times\ 5 \\ \hline 30 \end{array}$
2) $\begin{array}{r} \square \\ \times\ 2 \\ \hline 10 \end{array}$
3) $\begin{array}{r} \square \\ \times\ 3 \\ \hline 12 \end{array}$
4) $\begin{array}{r} \square \\ \times\ 4 \\ \hline 32 \end{array}$
5) $\begin{array}{r} \square \\ \times\ 3 \\ \hline 6 \end{array}$

6) $\begin{array}{r} \square \\ \times\ 8 \\ \hline 8 \end{array}$
7) $\begin{array}{r} \square \\ \times\ 3 \\ \hline 21 \end{array}$
8) $\begin{array}{r} \square \\ \times\ 9 \\ \hline 72 \end{array}$
9) $\begin{array}{r} \square \\ \times\ 6 \\ \hline 48 \end{array}$
10) $\begin{array}{r} \square \\ \times\ 7 \\ \hline 7 \end{array}$

11) $\begin{array}{r} \square \\ \times\ 8 \\ \hline 48 \end{array}$
12) $\begin{array}{r} \square \\ \times\ 3 \\ \hline 24 \end{array}$
13) $\begin{array}{r} \square \\ \times\ 5 \\ \hline 10 \end{array}$
14) $\begin{array}{r} \square \\ \times\ 1 \\ \hline 2 \end{array}$
15) $\begin{array}{r} \square \\ \times\ 1 \\ \hline 8 \end{array}$

16) $\begin{array}{r} \square \\ \times\ 7 \\ \hline 35 \end{array}$
17) $\begin{array}{r} \square \\ \times\ 7 \\ \hline 14 \end{array}$
18) $\begin{array}{r} \square \\ \times\ 9 \\ \hline 45 \end{array}$
19) $\begin{array}{r} \square \\ \times\ 6 \\ \hline 12 \end{array}$
20) $\begin{array}{r} \square \\ \times\ 2 \\ \hline 18 \end{array}$

21) $\begin{array}{r} \square \\ \times\ 3 \\ \hline 18 \end{array}$
22) $\begin{array}{r} \square \\ \times\ 3 \\ \hline 15 \end{array}$
23) $\begin{array}{r} \square \\ \times\ 8 \\ \hline 56 \end{array}$
24) $\begin{array}{r} \square \\ \times\ 5 \\ \hline 35 \end{array}$
25) $\begin{array}{r} \square \\ \times\ 5 \\ \hline 30 \end{array}$

26) $\begin{array}{r} \square \\ \times\ 7 \\ \hline 14 \end{array}$
27) $\begin{array}{r} \square \\ \times\ 5 \\ \hline 35 \end{array}$
28) $\begin{array}{r} \square \\ \times\ 9 \\ \hline 54 \end{array}$
29) $\begin{array}{r} \square \\ \times\ 7 \\ \hline 35 \end{array}$
30) $\begin{array}{r} \square \\ \times\ 6 \\ \hline 12 \end{array}$

31) $\begin{array}{r} \square \\ \times\ 7 \\ \hline 42 \end{array}$
32) $\begin{array}{r} \square \\ \times\ 4 \\ \hline 32 \end{array}$
33) $\begin{array}{r} \square \\ \times\ 1 \\ \hline 3 \end{array}$
34) $\begin{array}{r} \square \\ \times\ 7 \\ \hline 7 \end{array}$
35) $\begin{array}{r} \square \\ \times\ 2 \\ \hline 18 \end{array}$

36) $\begin{array}{r} \square \\ \times\ 7 \\ \hline 14 \end{array}$
37) $\begin{array}{r} \square \\ \times\ 6 \\ \hline 24 \end{array}$
38) $\begin{array}{r} \square \\ \times\ 5 \\ \hline 20 \end{array}$
39) $\begin{array}{r} \square \\ \times\ 3 \\ \hline 21 \end{array}$
40) $\begin{array}{r} \square \\ \times\ 9 \\ \hline 36 \end{array}$

1)
$\square$
$\times\ 9$
——
81

2)
$\square$
$\times\ 9$
——
63

3)
$\square$
$\times\ 4$
——
12

4)
$\square$
$\times\ 9$
——
18

5)
$\square$
$\times\ 6$
——
18

6)
$\square$
$\times\ 4$
——
8

7)
$\square$
$\times\ 9$
——
36

8)
$\square$
$\times\ 8$
——
40

9)
$\square$
$\times\ 9$
——
18

10)
$\square$
$\times\ 6$
——
54

11)
$\square$
$\times\ 5$
——
15

12)
$\square$
$\times\ 7$
——
63

13)
$\square$
$\times\ 2$
——
6

14)
$\square$
$\times\ 8$
——
8

15)
$\square$
$\times\ 2$
——
14

16)
$\square$
$\times\ 2$
——
14

17)
$\square$
$\times\ 8$
——
64

18)
$\square$
$\times\ 8$
——
64

19)
$\square$
$\times\ 4$
——
36

20)
$\square$
$\times\ 4$
——
8

21)
$\square$
$\times\ 6$
——
24

22)
$\square$
$\times\ 4$
——
8

23)
$\square$
$\times\ 1$
——
8

24)
$\square$
$\times\ 9$
——
45

25)
$\square$
$\times\ 8$
——
16

26)
$\square$
$\times\ 4$
——
8

27)
$\square$
$\times\ 3$
——
27

28)
$\square$
$\times\ 7$
——
56

29)
$\square$
$\times\ 6$
——
30

30)
$\square$
$\times\ 8$
——
56

31)
$\square$
$\times\ 4$
——
36

32)
$\square$
$\times\ 8$
——
48

33)
$\square$
$\times\ 7$
——
35

34)
$\square$
$\times\ 3$
——
18

35)
$\square$
$\times\ 3$
——
27

36)
$\square$
$\times\ 8$
——
40

37)
$\square$
$\times\ 9$
——
45

38)
$\square$
$\times\ 4$
——
28

39)
$\square$
$\times\ 9$
——
54

40)
$\square$
$\times\ 4$
——
36

1)
$$\begin{array}{r} \square \\ \times\ 8 \\ \hline 16 \end{array}$$

2)
$$\begin{array}{r} \square \\ \times\ 3 \\ \hline 18 \end{array}$$

3)
$$\begin{array}{r} \square \\ \times\ 8 \\ \hline 56 \end{array}$$

4)
$$\begin{array}{r} \square \\ \times\ 9 \\ \hline 9 \end{array}$$

5)
$$\begin{array}{r} \square \\ \times\ 4 \\ \hline 16 \end{array}$$

6)
$$\begin{array}{r} \square \\ \times\ 5 \\ \hline 15 \end{array}$$

7)
$$\begin{array}{r} \square \\ \times\ 4 \\ \hline 16 \end{array}$$

8)
$$\begin{array}{r} \square \\ \times\ 5 \\ \hline 25 \end{array}$$

9)
$$\begin{array}{r} \square \\ \times\ 8 \\ \hline 8 \end{array}$$

10)
$$\begin{array}{r} \square \\ \times\ 7 \\ \hline 14 \end{array}$$

11)
$$\begin{array}{r} \square \\ \times\ 3 \\ \hline 27 \end{array}$$

12)
$$\begin{array}{r} \square \\ \times\ 7 \\ \hline 49 \end{array}$$

13)
$$\begin{array}{r} \square \\ \times\ 9 \\ \hline 27 \end{array}$$

14)
$$\begin{array}{r} \square \\ \times\ 8 \\ \hline 64 \end{array}$$

15)
$$\begin{array}{r} \square \\ \times\ 4 \\ \hline 28 \end{array}$$

16)
$$\begin{array}{r} \square \\ \times\ 5 \\ \hline 40 \end{array}$$

17)
$$\begin{array}{r} \square \\ \times\ 5 \\ \hline 40 \end{array}$$

18)
$$\begin{array}{r} \square \\ \times\ 7 \\ \hline 21 \end{array}$$

19)
$$\begin{array}{r} \square \\ \times\ 7 \\ \hline 49 \end{array}$$

20)
$$\begin{array}{r} \square \\ \times\ 4 \\ \hline 28 \end{array}$$

21)
$$\begin{array}{r} \square \\ \times\ 2 \\ \hline 16 \end{array}$$

22)
$$\begin{array}{r} \square \\ \times\ 1 \\ \hline 4 \end{array}$$

23)
$$\begin{array}{r} \square \\ \times\ 6 \\ \hline 36 \end{array}$$

24)
$$\begin{array}{r} \square \\ \times\ 8 \\ \hline 32 \end{array}$$

25)
$$\begin{array}{r} \square \\ \times\ 1 \\ \hline 4 \end{array}$$

26)
$$\begin{array}{r} \square \\ \times\ 7 \\ \hline 49 \end{array}$$

27)
$$\begin{array}{r} \square \\ \times\ 5 \\ \hline 30 \end{array}$$

28)
$$\begin{array}{r} \square \\ \times\ 3 \\ \hline 24 \end{array}$$

29)
$$\begin{array}{r} \square \\ \times\ 4 \\ \hline 28 \end{array}$$

30)
$$\begin{array}{r} \square \\ \times\ 1 \\ \hline 1 \end{array}$$

31)
$$\begin{array}{r} \square \\ \times\ 2 \\ \hline 18 \end{array}$$

32)
$$\begin{array}{r} \square \\ \times\ 5 \\ \hline 5 \end{array}$$

33)
$$\begin{array}{r} \square \\ \times\ 2 \\ \hline 8 \end{array}$$

34)
$$\begin{array}{r} \square \\ \times\ 3 \\ \hline 12 \end{array}$$

35)
$$\begin{array}{r} \square \\ \times\ 7 \\ \hline 56 \end{array}$$

36)
$$\begin{array}{r} \square \\ \times\ 8 \\ \hline 64 \end{array}$$

37)
$$\begin{array}{r} \square \\ \times\ 7 \\ \hline 21 \end{array}$$

38)
$$\begin{array}{r} \square \\ \times\ 1 \\ \hline 2 \end{array}$$

39)
$$\begin{array}{r} \square \\ \times\ 1 \\ \hline 7 \end{array}$$

40)
$$\begin{array}{r} \square \\ \times\ 5 \\ \hline 30 \end{array}$$

1) $3 \times \square = 3$

2) $4 \times \square = 24$

3) $1 \times \square = 2$

4) $9 \times \square = 72$

5) $7 \times \square = 56$

6) $1 \times \square = 7$

7) $2 \times \square = 14$

8) $7 \times \square = 21$

9) $9 \times \square = 45$

10) $9 \times \square = 72$

11) $4 \times \square = 8$

12) $2 \times \square = 16$

13) $5 \times \square = 25$

14) $4 \times \square = 12$

15) $7 \times \square = 21$

16) $8 \times \square = 64$

17) $7 \times \square = 35$

18) $7 \times \square = 49$

19) $4 \times \square = 4$

20) $5 \times \square = 30$

21) $2 \times \square = 2$

22) $5 \times \square = 25$

23) $6 \times \square = 12$

24) $4 \times \square = 8$

25) $2 \times \square = 16$

26) $6 \times \square = 30$

27) $6 \times \square = 42$

28) $6 \times \square = 42$

29) $3 \times \square = 21$

30) $8 \times \square = 40$

31) $8 \times \square = 64$

32) $7 \times \square = 35$

33) $4 \times \square = 24$

34) $4 \times \square = 20$

35) $1 \times \square = 5$

36) $3 \times \square = 15$

37) $4 \times \square = 24$

38) $4 \times \square = 12$

39) $2 \times \square = 14$

40) $7 \times \square = 21$

1) $9 \times \square = 63$

2) $7 \times \square = 14$

3) $2 \times \square = 10$

4) $5 \times \square = 30$

5) $1 \times \square = 9$

6) $3 \times \square = 24$

7) $4 \times \square = 36$

8) $8 \times \square = 72$

9) $1 \times \square = 9$

10) $4 \times \square = 24$

11) $7 \times \square = 28$

12) $1 \times \square = 2$

13) $6 \times \square = 48$

14) $3 \times \square = 18$

15) $5 \times \square = 30$

16) $1 \times \square = 1$

17) $9 \times \square = 54$

18) $9 \times \square = 9$

19) $8 \times \square = 32$

20) $1 \times \square = 4$

21) $8 \times \square = 24$

22) $9 \times \square = 45$

23) $5 \times \square = 10$

24) $3 \times \square = 27$

25) $4 \times \square = 24$

26) $1 \times \square = 7$

27) $8 \times \square = 56$

28) $7 \times \square = 35$

29) $2 \times \square = 10$

30) $2 \times \square = 18$

31) $8 \times \square = 72$

32) $5 \times \square = 30$

33) $5 \times \square = 35$

34) $5 \times \square = 10$

35) $5 \times \square = 30$

36) $1 \times \square = 3$

37) $7 \times \square = 42$

38) $5 \times \square = 25$

39) $8 \times \square = 40$

40) $7 \times \square = 56$

Day 26

TIME:

DATE:

SCORE: /

29

1) 4 × ☐ = 8

2) 6 × ☐ = 18

3) 8 × ☐ = 64

4) 7 × ☐ = 49

5) 3 × ☐ = 9

6) 8 × ☐ = 32

7) 3 × ☐ = 3

8) 4 × ☐ = 28

9) 4 × ☐ = 32

10) 4 × ☐ = 20

11) 5 × ☐ = 25

12) 5 × ☐ = 20

13) 5 × ☐ = 20

14) 2 × ☐ = 12

15) 6 × ☐ = 54

16) 4 × ☐ = 20

17) 3 × ☐ = 6

18) 2 × ☐ = 8

19) 5 × ☐ = 15

20) 3 × ☐ = 9

21) 8 × ☐ = 32

22) 9 × ☐ = 54

23) 9 × ☐ = 63

24) 2 × ☐ = 18

25) 1 × ☐ = 4

26) 8 × ☐ = 40

27) 5 × ☐ = 10

28) 3 × ☐ = 6

29) 4 × ☐ = 16

30) 7 × ☐ = 21

31) 2 × ☐ = 4

32) 5 × ☐ = 10

33) 1 × ☐ = 9

34) 8 × ☐ = 24

35) 1 × ☐ = 6

36) 3 × ☐ = 9

37) 9 × ☐ = 36

38) 1 × ☐ = 3

39) 3 × ☐ = 15

40) 2 × ☐ = 16

1) $21 \div 3 = $

2) $95 \div 5 = $

3) $36 \div 4 = $

4) $16 \div 8 = $

5) $42 \div 7 = $

6) $92 \div 2 = $

7) $50 \div 2 = $

8) $52 \div 4 = $

9) $48 \div 3 = $

10) $16 \div 8 = $

11) $16 \div 4 = $

12) $96 \div 6 = $

13) $84 \div 3 = $

14) $52 \div 2 = $

15) $14 \div 2 = $

16) $27 \div 3 = $

17) $84 \div 3 = $

18) $35 \div 7 = $

19) $65 \div 5 = $

20) $12 \div 6 = $

21) $30 \div 6 = $

22) $58 \div 2 = $

23) $56 \div 2 = $

24) $64 \div 8 = $

25) $96 \div 4 = $

26) $58 \div 2 = $

27) $54 \div 6 = $

28) $78 \div 3 = $

29) $12 \div 4 = $

30) $48 \div 3 = $

31) $36 \div 6 = $

32) $54 \div 2 = $

33) $12 \div 3 = $

34) $27 \div 9 = $

35) $28 \div 7 = $

36) $20 \div 4 = $

37) $90 \div 6 = $

38) $45 \div 3 = $

39) $70 \div 2 = $

40) $87 \div 3 = $

1) $28 \div 4$

2) $79 \div 1$

3) $82 \div 1$

4) $18 \div 6$

5) $65 \div 1$

6) $1 \div 1$

7) $19 \div 1$

8) $10 \div 1$

9) $81 \div 1$

10) $21 \div 3$

11) $19 \div 1$

12) $86 \div 1$

13) $56 \div 1$

14) $91 \div 7$

15) $84 \div 1$

16) $3 \div 1$

17) $21 \div 3$

18) $4 \div 1$

19) $89 \div 1$

20) $84 \div 6$

21) $55 \div 5$

22) $70 \div 1$

23) $49 \div 1$

24) $64 \div 8$

25) $6 \div 3$

26) $67 \div 1$

27) $43 \div 1$

28) $82 \div 2$

29) $7 \div 7$

30) $72 \div 1$

31) $48 \div 3$

32) $92 \div 4$

33) $60 \div 5$

34) $26 \div 2$

35) $39 \div 1$

36) $54 \div 9$

37) $73 \div 1$

38) $61 \div 1$

39) $38 \div 1$

40) $73 \div 1$

1) 97 ÷ 1

2) 8 ÷ 8

3) 73 ÷ 1

4) 92 ÷ 2

5) 56 ÷ 4

6) 64 ÷ 8

7) 87 ÷ 3

8) 53 ÷ 1

9) 47 ÷ 1

10) 25 ÷ 1

11) 7 ÷ 1

12) 57 ÷ 1

13) 78 ÷ 1

14) 13 ÷ 1

15) 63 ÷ 7

16) 44 ÷ 2

17) 4 ÷ 2

18) 96 ÷ 6

19) 91 ÷ 7

20) 7 ÷ 7

21) 20 ÷ 1

22) 48 ÷ 3

23) 91 ÷ 1

24) 24 ÷ 1

25) 37 ÷ 1

26) 44 ÷ 1

27) 30 ÷ 1

28) 74 ÷ 2

29) 53 ÷ 1

30) 39 ÷ 1

31) 53 ÷ 1

32) 27 ÷ 9

33) 49 ÷ 1

34) 18 ÷ 1

35) 9 ÷ 3

36) 44 ÷ 2

37) 80 ÷ 8

38) 71 ÷ 1

39) 39 ÷ 1

40) 85 ÷ 1

1) $51 \div 3$

2) $3 \div 1$

3) $87 \div 3$

4) $89 \div 1$

5) $56 \div 8$

6) $100 \div 4$

7) $27 \div 1$

8) $84 \div 2$

9) $90 \div 1$

10) $56 \div 1$

11) $81 \div 9$

12) $57 \div 3$

13) $45 \div 3$

14) $68 \div 4$

15) $70 \div 2$

16) $61 \div 1$

17) $38 \div 1$

18) $96 \div 4$

19) $12 \div 3$

20) $28 \div 4$

21) $52 \div 2$

22) $37 \div 1$

23) $60 \div 1$

24) $49 \div 7$

25) $57 \div 1$

26) $26 \div 2$

27) $76 \div 2$

28) $86 \div 1$

29) $48 \div 1$

30) $42 \div 6$

31) $49 \div 1$

32) $15 \div 3$

33) $97 \div 1$

34) $10 \div 1$

35) $32 \div 4$

36) $64 \div 1$

37) $42 \div 1$

38) $100 \div 1$

39) $100 \div 5$

40) $38 \div 1$

1) $\div \dfrac{\boxed{}\quad 1}{37}$
2) $\div \dfrac{\boxed{}\quad 1}{81}$
3) $\div \dfrac{\boxed{}\quad 9}{6}$
4) $\div \dfrac{\boxed{}\quad 7}{3}$
5) $\div \dfrac{\boxed{}\quad 3}{27}$

6) $\div \dfrac{\boxed{}\quad 2}{7}$
7) $\div \dfrac{\boxed{}\quad 7}{2}$
8) $\div \dfrac{\boxed{}\quad 9}{6}$
9) $\div \dfrac{\boxed{}\quad 7}{5}$
10) $\div \dfrac{\boxed{}\quad 1}{7}$

11) $\div \dfrac{\boxed{}\quad 1}{29}$
12) $\div \dfrac{\boxed{}\quad 5}{5}$
13) $\div \dfrac{\boxed{}\quad 1}{11}$
14) $\div \dfrac{\boxed{}\quad 1}{94}$
15) $\div \dfrac{\boxed{}\quad 9}{7}$

16) $\div \dfrac{\boxed{}\quad 9}{9}$
17) $\div \dfrac{\boxed{}\quad 1}{42}$
18) $\div \dfrac{\boxed{}\quad 1}{54}$
19) $\div \dfrac{\boxed{}\quad 1}{99}$
20) $\div \dfrac{\boxed{}\quad 1}{59}$

21) $\div \dfrac{\boxed{}\quad 1}{65}$
22) $\div \dfrac{\boxed{}\quad 5}{15}$
23) $\div \dfrac{\boxed{}\quad 1}{81}$
24) $\div \dfrac{\boxed{}\quad 1}{73}$
25) $\div \dfrac{\boxed{}\quad 2}{47}$

26) $\div \dfrac{\boxed{}\quad 9}{1}$
27) $\div \dfrac{\boxed{}\quad 7}{5}$
28) $\div \dfrac{\boxed{}\quad 2}{20}$
29) $\div \dfrac{\boxed{}\quad 2}{7}$
30) $\div \dfrac{\boxed{}\quad 1}{76}$

31) $\div \dfrac{\boxed{}\quad 5}{13}$
32) $\div \dfrac{\boxed{}\quad 2}{26}$
33) $\div \dfrac{\boxed{}\quad 2}{19}$
34) $\div \dfrac{\boxed{}\quad 1}{73}$
35) $\div \dfrac{\boxed{}\quad 2}{41}$

36) $\div \dfrac{\boxed{}\quad 1}{52}$
37) $\div \dfrac{\boxed{}\quad 3}{32}$
38) $\div \dfrac{\boxed{}\quad 4}{3}$
39) $\div \dfrac{\boxed{}\quad 5}{10}$
40) $\div \dfrac{\boxed{}\quad 1}{49}$

1) □ ÷ 1 / 58

2) □ ÷ 1 / 98

3) □ ÷ 1 / 4

4) □ ÷ 2 / 37

5) □ ÷ 9 / 8

6) □ ÷ 4 / 12

7) □ ÷ 7 / 7

8) □ ÷ 1 / 1

9) □ ÷ 1 / 69

10) □ ÷ 3 / 32

11) □ ÷ 1 / 74

12) □ ÷ 1 / 85

13) □ ÷ 2 / 31

14) □ ÷ 1 / 30

15) □ ÷ 1 / 78

16) □ ÷ 2 / 41

17) □ ÷ 1 / 11

18) □ ÷ 1 / 69

19) □ ÷ 1 / 2

20) □ ÷ 1 / 43

21) □ ÷ 1 / 34

22) □ ÷ 1 / 14

23) □ ÷ 5 / 10

24) □ ÷ 5 / 10

25) □ ÷ 1 / 55

26) □ ÷ 4 / 13

27) □ ÷ 1 / 23

28) □ ÷ 4 / 8

29) □ ÷ 4 / 10

30) □ ÷ 4 / 5

31) □ ÷ 1 / 77

32) □ ÷ 4 / 1

33) □ ÷ 1 / 79

34) □ ÷ 3 / 19

35) □ ÷ 1 / 28

36) □ ÷ 8 / 5

37) □ ÷ 1 / 31

38) □ ÷ 9 / 1

39) □ ÷ 1 / 73

40) □ ÷ 1 / 65

1) $80 \div \square = 10$

2) $34 \div \square = 17$

3) $59 \div \square = 59$

4) $26 \div \square = 26$

5) $83 \div \square = 83$

6) $60 \div \square = 10$

7) $61 \div \square = 61$

8) $31 \div \square = 31$

9) $76 \div \square = 38$

10) $52 \div \square = 52$

11) $9 \div \square = 1$

12) $2 \div \square = 2$

13) $71 \div \square = 71$

14) $74 \div \square = 37$

15) $8 \div \square = 4$

16) $67 \div \square = 67$

17) $78 \div \square = 39$

18) $53 \div \square = 53$

19) $1 \div \square = 1$

20) $29 \div \square = 29$

21) $54 \div \square = 27$

22) $92 \div \square = 46$

23) $99 \div \square = 33$

24) $83 \div \square = 83$

25) $68 \div \square = 34$

26) $4 \div \square = 1$

27) $65 \div \square = 65$

28) $99 \div \square = 99$

29) $1 \div \square = 1$

30) $90 \div \square = 15$

31) $25 \div \square = 25$

32) $96 \div \square = 24$

33) $81 \div \square = 81$

34) $7 \div \square = 7$

35) $88 \div \square = 44$

36) $40 \div \square = 20$

37) $8 \div \square = 8$

38) $44 \div \square = 22$

39) $50 \div \square = 25$

40) $69 \div \square = 23$

1) 51 ÷ □ = 17

2) 38 ÷ □ = 38

3) 81 ÷ □ = 81

4) 33 ÷ □ = 11

5) 83 ÷ □ = 83

6) 94 ÷ □ = 94

7) 39 ÷ □ = 13

8) 21 ÷ □ = 7

9) 99 ÷ □ = 33

10) 24 ÷ □ = 3

11) 44 ÷ □ = 11

12) 42 ÷ □ = 7

13) 90 ÷ □ = 30

14) 88 ÷ □ = 44

15) 91 ÷ □ = 13

16) 3 ÷ □ = 1

17) 96 ÷ □ = 96

18) 89 ÷ □ = 89

19) 5 ÷ □ = 1

20) 9 ÷ □ = 1

21) 52 ÷ □ = 26

22) 72 ÷ □ = 9

23) 43 ÷ □ = 43

24) 94 ÷ □ = 94

25) 68 ÷ □ = 17

26) 57 ÷ □ = 19

27) 88 ÷ □ = 44

28) 18 ÷ □ = 3

29) 36 ÷ □ = 12

30) 72 ÷ □ = 9

31) 68 ÷ □ = 34

32) 67 ÷ □ = 67

33) 46 ÷ □ = 46

34) 72 ÷ □ = 36

35) 3 ÷ □ = 1

36) 79 ÷ □ = 79

37) 59 ÷ □ = 59

38) 35 ÷ □ = 5

39) 66 ÷ □ = 22

40) 77 ÷ □ = 77

1) $52 \div \square = 13$

2) $28 \div \square = 4$

3) $57 \div \square = 19$

4) $45 \div \square = 15$

5) $63 \div \square = 21$

6) $55 \div \square = 11$

7) $77 \div \square = 77$

8) $57 \div \square = 19$

9) $12 \div \square = 3$

10) $24 \div \square = 4$

11) $97 \div \square = 97$

12) $74 \div \square = 74$

13) $13 \div \square = 13$

14) $41 \div \square = 41$

15) $77 \div \square = 11$

16) $3 \div \square = 1$

17) $40 \div \square = 40$

18) $12 \div \square = 6$

19) $89 \div \square = 89$

20) $81 \div \square = 27$

21) $37 \div \square = 37$

22) $34 \div \square = 17$

23) $31 \div \square = 31$

24) $19 \div \square = 19$

25) $11 \div \square = 11$

26) $38 \div \square = 19$

27) $69 \div \square = 23$

28) $81 \div \square = 81$

29) $55 \div \square = 55$

30) $64 \div \square = 64$

31) $12 \div \square = 3$

32) $29 \div \square = 29$

33) $87 \div \square = 87$

34) $54 \div \square = 18$

35) $71 \div \square = 71$

36) $37 \div \square = 37$

37) $82 \div \square = 41$

38) $69 \div \square = 23$

39) $21 \div \square = 21$

40) $64 \div \square = 32$

1) $1 \overline{)2\,5}$

2) $2 \overline{)7\,4}$

3) $5 \overline{)1\,5}$

4) $5 \overline{)1\,5}$

5) $1 \overline{)1\,8}$

6) $8 \overline{)9\,6}$

1) $5 \overline{)8\ 5}$

2) $2 \overline{)7\ 4}$

3) $2 \overline{)5\ 0}$

4) $2 \overline{)5\ 0}$

5) $2 \overline{)7\ 6}$

6) $3 \overline{)1\ 8}$

1)

Half past

2)

Half past

3)

Half past

4)

Half past

5)

Half past

6)

Half past

7)

Half past

8)

Half past

9)

Half past

1)

Half past ⌐ ‾ ‾ ‾ ‾ ¬

2)

Half past ⌐ ‾ ‾ ‾ ‾ ¬

3)

Half past ⌐ ‾ ‾ ‾ ‾ ¬

4)

Half past ⌐ ‾ ‾ ‾ ‾ ¬

5)

Half past ⌐ ‾ ‾ ‾ ‾ ¬

6)

Half past ⌐ ‾ ‾ ‾ ‾ ¬

7)

Half past ⌐ ‾ ‾ ‾ ‾ ¬

8)

Half past ⌐ ‾ ‾ ‾ ‾ ¬

9)

Half past ⌐ ‾ ‾ ‾ ‾ ¬

1)

.... o'clock

2)

.... o'clock

3)

.... o'clock

4)

.... o'clock

5)

.... o'clock

6)

.... o'clock

7)

.... o'clock

8)

.... o'clock

9)

.... o'clock

1)

Quarter past   9:00

2)

Quarter past   8:00

3)

Quarter past   5:00

4)

Quarter past   5:00

5)

Quarter past   11:00

6)

Quarter past   4:00

7)

Quarter past   1:00

8)

Quarter past   7:00

9)

Quarter past   4:00

TIME:

DATE:

SCORE:
/

1)

Quarter past   9:00

2)

Quarter past   2:00

3)

Quarter past   2:00

4)

Quarter past   1:00

5)

Quarter past   2:00

6)

Quarter past   3:00

7)

Quarter past   5:00

8)

Quarter past   5:00

9)

Quarter past   2:00

1) $\dfrac{4}{9} + \dfrac{1}{9} =$

2) $\dfrac{4}{5} + \dfrac{2}{5} =$

3) $\dfrac{5}{8} + \dfrac{2}{8} =$

4) $\dfrac{5}{10} + \dfrac{8}{10} =$

5) $\dfrac{5}{7} + \dfrac{6}{7} =$

6) $\dfrac{2}{8} + \dfrac{2}{8} =$

7) $\dfrac{1}{7} + \dfrac{5}{7} =$

8) $\dfrac{3}{9} + \dfrac{6}{9} =$

9) $\dfrac{1}{9} + \dfrac{1}{9} =$

10) $\dfrac{4}{8} + \dfrac{3}{8} =$

11) $\dfrac{5}{9} + \dfrac{5}{9} =$

12) $\dfrac{4}{8} + \dfrac{7}{8} =$

13) $\dfrac{3}{8} + \dfrac{3}{8} =$

14) $\dfrac{5}{9} + \dfrac{2}{9} =$

15) $\dfrac{2}{6} + \dfrac{5}{6} =$

16) $\dfrac{8}{9} + \dfrac{5}{9} =$

17) $\dfrac{4}{8} + \dfrac{1}{8} =$

18) $\dfrac{4}{9} + \dfrac{7}{9} =$

19) $\dfrac{6}{7} + \dfrac{3}{7} =$

20) $\dfrac{5}{10} + \dfrac{9}{10} =$

21) $\dfrac{5}{8} + \dfrac{6}{8} =$

22) $\dfrac{2}{4} + \dfrac{1}{4} =$

23) $\dfrac{6}{8} + \dfrac{5}{8} =$

24) $\dfrac{2}{9} + \dfrac{7}{9} =$

1) $\dfrac{5}{7} + \dfrac{1}{7} =$

2) $\dfrac{5}{10} + \dfrac{8}{10} =$

3) $\dfrac{1}{4} + \dfrac{1}{4} =$

4) $\dfrac{4}{7} + \dfrac{1}{7} =$

5) $\dfrac{1}{9} + \dfrac{1}{9} =$

6) $\dfrac{3}{4} + \dfrac{1}{4} =$

7) $\dfrac{5}{7} + \dfrac{2}{7} =$

8) $\dfrac{3}{10} + \dfrac{2}{10} =$

9) $\dfrac{2}{7} + \dfrac{6}{7} =$

10) $\dfrac{2}{6} + \dfrac{4}{6} =$

11) $\dfrac{1}{4} + \dfrac{3}{4} =$

12) $\dfrac{6}{9} + \dfrac{3}{9} =$

13) $\dfrac{3}{5} + \dfrac{2}{5} =$

14) $\dfrac{4}{8} + \dfrac{5}{8} =$

15) $\dfrac{4}{10} + \dfrac{3}{10} =$

16) $\dfrac{3}{5} + \dfrac{3}{5} =$

17) $\dfrac{1}{4} + \dfrac{2}{4} =$

18) $\dfrac{8}{10} + \dfrac{4}{10} =$

19) $\dfrac{7}{9} + \dfrac{6}{9} =$

20) $\dfrac{4}{8} + \dfrac{4}{8} =$

21) $\dfrac{7}{9} + \dfrac{3}{9} =$

22) $\dfrac{3}{8} + \dfrac{5}{8} =$

23) $\dfrac{1}{3} + \dfrac{2}{3} =$

24) $\dfrac{4}{10} + \dfrac{8}{10} =$

TIME:

DATE:

SCORE: /

48

1) $\dfrac{5}{9} + \dfrac{5}{9} =$

2) $\dfrac{1}{3} + \dfrac{1}{7} =$

3) $\dfrac{2}{4} + \dfrac{1}{6} =$

4) $\dfrac{8}{10} + \dfrac{3}{7} =$

5) $\dfrac{9}{10} + \dfrac{1}{5} =$

6) $\dfrac{2}{7} + \dfrac{2}{7} =$

7) $\dfrac{4}{8} + \dfrac{9}{10} =$

8) $\dfrac{5}{8} + \dfrac{6}{9} =$

9) $\dfrac{4}{6} + \dfrac{1}{6} =$

10) $\dfrac{3}{4} + \dfrac{5}{8} =$

11) $\dfrac{3}{8} + \dfrac{2}{8} =$

12) $\dfrac{4}{7} + \dfrac{2}{10} =$

13) $\dfrac{9}{10} + \dfrac{5}{10} =$

14) $\dfrac{1}{4} + \dfrac{8}{10} =$

15) $\dfrac{4}{6} + \dfrac{3}{9} =$

16) $\dfrac{6}{9} + \dfrac{4}{6} =$

17) $\dfrac{3}{8} + \dfrac{1}{4} =$

18) $\dfrac{2}{7} + \dfrac{1}{7} =$

19) $\dfrac{9}{10} + \dfrac{1}{9} =$

20) $\dfrac{6}{7} + \dfrac{1}{3} =$

21) $\dfrac{1}{8} + \dfrac{4}{8} =$

22) $\dfrac{4}{8} + \dfrac{1}{8} =$

23) $\dfrac{3}{10} + \dfrac{1}{8} =$

24) $\dfrac{4}{5} + \dfrac{6}{8} =$

1) $\dfrac{2}{6} + \dfrac{1}{7} =$

2) $\dfrac{2}{6} + \dfrac{5}{6} =$

3) $\dfrac{5}{8} + \dfrac{2}{7} =$

4) $\dfrac{4}{7} + \dfrac{2}{7} =$

5) $\dfrac{2}{8} + \dfrac{7}{9} =$

6) $\dfrac{2}{3} + \dfrac{5}{9} =$

7) $\dfrac{4}{10} + \dfrac{7}{10} =$

8) $\dfrac{3}{4} + \dfrac{6}{10} =$

9) $\dfrac{5}{6} + \dfrac{8}{9} =$

10) $\dfrac{3}{9} + \dfrac{6}{9} =$

11) $\dfrac{3}{7} + \dfrac{3}{5} =$

12) $\dfrac{1}{8} + \dfrac{5}{9} =$

13) $\dfrac{4}{10} + \dfrac{6}{10} =$

14) $\dfrac{4}{9} + \dfrac{2}{4} =$

15) $\dfrac{1}{8} + \dfrac{1}{6} =$

16) $\dfrac{6}{8} + \dfrac{2}{8} =$

17) $\dfrac{3}{4} + \dfrac{6}{10} =$

18) $\dfrac{5}{7} + \dfrac{5}{10} =$

19) $\dfrac{8}{9} + \dfrac{7}{9} =$

20) $\dfrac{1}{7} + \dfrac{2}{4} =$

21) $\dfrac{3}{10} + \dfrac{6}{10} =$

22) $\dfrac{3}{8} + \dfrac{5}{9} =$

23) $\dfrac{4}{7} + \dfrac{2}{4} =$

24) $\dfrac{1}{4} + \dfrac{2}{4} =$

1) $\dfrac{7}{4} + \dfrac{1}{4} =$

2) $\dfrac{9}{8} + \dfrac{4}{9} =$

3) $\dfrac{9}{7} + \dfrac{8}{10} =$

4) $\dfrac{8}{9} + \dfrac{7}{9} =$

5) $5 + \dfrac{5}{8} =$

6) $5 + \dfrac{1}{3} =$

7) $\dfrac{9}{3} + \dfrac{3}{10} =$

8) $\dfrac{9}{6} + \dfrac{6}{8} =$

9) $\dfrac{3}{9} + \dfrac{5}{9} =$

10) $\dfrac{6}{7} + \dfrac{2}{4} =$

11) $\dfrac{4}{3} + \dfrac{6}{8} =$

12) $\dfrac{10}{8} + \dfrac{2}{8}$

13) $\dfrac{1}{5} + \dfrac{3}{7} =$

14) $\dfrac{6}{10} + \dfrac{6}{10} =$

15) $\dfrac{7}{9} + \dfrac{2}{9} =$

16) $\dfrac{2}{10} + \dfrac{7}{10} =$

17) $6 + \dfrac{5}{8} =$

18) $\dfrac{10}{8} + \dfrac{8}{10}$

19) $\dfrac{10}{7} + \dfrac{6}{7} =$

20) $4 + \dfrac{3}{9} =$

21) $\dfrac{5}{3} + \dfrac{3}{8} =$

22) $\dfrac{4}{6} + \dfrac{3}{6} =$

23) $\dfrac{8}{7} + \dfrac{1}{5} =$

24) $\dfrac{6}{8} + \dfrac{6}{10} =$

1) $\dfrac{5}{5} + \dfrac{2}{5} =$

2) $\dfrac{3}{6} + \dfrac{3}{8} =$

3) $\dfrac{8}{4} + \dfrac{3}{4} =$

4) $\dfrac{3}{3} + \dfrac{2}{3} =$

5) $\dfrac{7}{4} + \dfrac{1}{5} =$

6) $\dfrac{9}{9} + \dfrac{3}{10} =$

7) $\dfrac{4}{7} + \dfrac{7}{8} =$

8) $\dfrac{9}{6} + \dfrac{3}{6} =$

9) $\dfrac{6}{9} + \dfrac{8}{10} =$

10) $6 + \dfrac{6}{9} =$

11) $\dfrac{10}{5} + \dfrac{4}{9} =$

12) $\dfrac{10}{4} + \dfrac{1}{4}$

13) $\dfrac{2}{5} + \dfrac{1}{3} =$

14) $\dfrac{2}{4} + \dfrac{2}{4} =$

15) $\dfrac{8}{4} + \dfrac{3}{7} =$

16) $\dfrac{2}{10} + \dfrac{4}{10} =$

17) $\dfrac{9}{9} + \dfrac{1}{9} =$

18) $\dfrac{4}{8} + \dfrac{2}{9} =$

19) $\dfrac{8}{9} + \dfrac{4}{5} =$

20) $\dfrac{10}{9} + \dfrac{5}{10} =$

21) $\dfrac{9}{3} + \dfrac{2}{3} =$

22) $\dfrac{2}{3} + \dfrac{2}{3} =$

23) $\dfrac{6}{4} + \dfrac{6}{7} =$

24) $\dfrac{4}{10} + \dfrac{3}{10} =$

1) $\dfrac{4}{7} + \dfrac{2}{7} =$ 2) $\dfrac{10}{4} + \dfrac{2}{9} =$ 3) $\dfrac{4}{6} + \dfrac{2}{10} =$

4) $\dfrac{1}{3} + \dfrac{3}{9} =$ 5) $\dfrac{10}{7} + \dfrac{3}{6} =$ 6) $\dfrac{1}{6} + \dfrac{5}{6} =$

7) $\dfrac{5}{8} + \dfrac{2}{6} =$ 8) $\dfrac{5}{10} + \dfrac{2}{4} =$ 9) $\dfrac{8}{9} + \dfrac{8}{9} =$

10) $\dfrac{10}{10} + \dfrac{7}{8} =$ 11) $\dfrac{6}{7} + \dfrac{3}{7} =$ 12) $\dfrac{3}{6} + \dfrac{1}{9} =$

13) $\dfrac{6}{8} + \dfrac{1}{7} =$ 14) $\dfrac{6}{9} + \dfrac{1}{8} =$ 15) $\dfrac{3}{8} + \dfrac{1}{8} =$

16) $\dfrac{9}{3} + \dfrac{1}{3} =$ 17) $\dfrac{7}{10} + \dfrac{1}{5} =$ 18) $\dfrac{1}{4} + \dfrac{8}{9} =$

19) $\dfrac{5}{3} + \dfrac{2}{4} =$ 20) $\dfrac{6}{10} + \dfrac{5}{7} =$ 21) $\dfrac{3}{5} + \dfrac{4}{5} =$

22) $\dfrac{10}{9} + \dfrac{3}{5} =$ 23) $\dfrac{4}{10} + \dfrac{2}{10} =$ 24) $\dfrac{8}{4} + \dfrac{1}{4} =$

1) $4\frac{4}{6} + 10\frac{1}{6} =$

2) $\frac{2}{10} + 10\frac{3}{10} =$

3) $\frac{5}{8} + 8\frac{7}{8} =$

4) $5\frac{1}{8} + 8\frac{6}{8} =$

5) $9\frac{7}{8} + 6\frac{5}{8} =$

6) $5\frac{3}{9} + 6\frac{5}{9} =$

7) $4\frac{7}{9} + 7\frac{2}{9} =$

8) $6\frac{5}{8} + 6\frac{6}{8} =$

9) $8\frac{5}{7} + 5\frac{3}{7} =$

10) $6\frac{8}{10} + 6\frac{3}{10} =$

11) $8\frac{5}{9} + 8\frac{8}{9} =$

12) $5\frac{1}{3} + 4\frac{2}{3} =$

13) $9\frac{5}{7} + 6\frac{1}{7} =$

14) $\frac{10}{8} + 7\frac{7}{8} =$

15) $5\frac{1}{9} + 6\frac{5}{9} =$

16) $5\frac{2}{7} + 6\frac{2}{7} =$

1) $4\frac{7}{9} + 4\frac{8}{9} =$

2) $6\frac{4}{6} + 10\frac{2}{6} =$

3) $9\frac{2}{7} + 10\frac{1}{7} =$

4) $\frac{5}{7} + 7\frac{3}{7} =$

5) $\frac{2}{6} + 6\frac{1}{6} =$

6) $7\frac{3}{8} + 10\frac{2}{8} =$

7) $\frac{9}{10} + 5\frac{6}{10} =$

8) $10\frac{4}{6} + 9\frac{2}{6} =$

9) $8\frac{6}{8} + 9\frac{1}{8} =$

10) $8\frac{8}{9} + 8\frac{4}{9} =$

11) $8\frac{5}{6} + 5\frac{1}{6} =$

12) $\frac{2}{7} + 4\frac{3}{7} =$

13) $7\frac{4}{9} + 8\frac{5}{9} =$

14) $\frac{8}{3} + 10\frac{1}{3} =$

15) $\frac{6}{5} + 4\frac{1}{5} =$

16) $4\frac{3}{7} + 4\frac{3}{7} =$

1) $\dfrac{5}{6} - \dfrac{2}{6} =$

2) $\dfrac{4}{5} - \dfrac{4}{5} =$

3) $\dfrac{5}{9} - \dfrac{3}{9} =$

4) $\dfrac{2}{5} - \dfrac{2}{5} =$

5) $\dfrac{6}{10} - \dfrac{6}{10} =$

6) $\dfrac{6}{7} - \dfrac{3}{7} =$

7) $\dfrac{8}{10} - \dfrac{3}{10} =$

8) $\dfrac{4}{6} - \dfrac{3}{6} =$

9) $\dfrac{7}{9} - \dfrac{7}{9} =$

10) $\dfrac{8}{10} - \dfrac{8}{10} =$

11) $\dfrac{3}{9} - \dfrac{1}{9} =$

12) $\dfrac{6}{10} - \dfrac{1}{10} =$

13) $\dfrac{7}{10} - \dfrac{3}{10} =$

14) $\dfrac{5}{10} - \dfrac{1}{10} =$

15) $\dfrac{7}{8} - \dfrac{3}{8} =$

16) $\dfrac{4}{9} - \dfrac{2}{9} =$

17) $\dfrac{7}{10} - \dfrac{6}{10} =$

18) $\dfrac{6}{8} - \dfrac{6}{8} =$

19) $\dfrac{5}{10} - \dfrac{2}{10} =$

20) $\dfrac{5}{10} - \dfrac{5}{10} =$

21) $\dfrac{2}{6} - \dfrac{2}{6} =$

22) $\dfrac{7}{8} - \dfrac{4}{8} =$

23) $\dfrac{3}{9} - \dfrac{3}{9} =$

24) $\dfrac{2}{8} - \dfrac{2}{8} =$

1) $\dfrac{3}{4} - \dfrac{3}{4} =$

2) $\dfrac{9}{10} - \dfrac{3}{10} =$

3) $\dfrac{7}{9} - \dfrac{4}{9} =$

4) $\dfrac{2}{5} - \dfrac{1}{5} =$

5) $\dfrac{2}{7} - \dfrac{2}{7} =$

6) $\dfrac{1}{5} - \dfrac{1}{5} =$

7) $\dfrac{8}{10} - \dfrac{7}{10} =$

8) $\dfrac{4}{7} - \dfrac{3}{7} =$

9) $\dfrac{2}{6} - \dfrac{1}{6} =$

10) $\dfrac{1}{3} - \dfrac{1}{3} =$

11) $\dfrac{5}{9} - \dfrac{3}{9} =$

12) $\dfrac{2}{9} - \dfrac{2}{9} =$

13) $\dfrac{9}{10} - \dfrac{6}{10} =$

14) $\dfrac{5}{8} - \dfrac{5}{8} =$

15) $\dfrac{7}{9} - \dfrac{2}{9} =$

16) $\dfrac{6}{9} - \dfrac{3}{9} =$

17) $\dfrac{3}{10} - \dfrac{2}{10} =$

18) $\dfrac{5}{9} - \dfrac{4}{9} =$

19) $\dfrac{5}{6} - \dfrac{4}{6} =$

20) $\dfrac{5}{10} - \dfrac{4}{10} =$

21) $\dfrac{4}{7} - \dfrac{2}{7} =$

22) $\dfrac{6}{9} - \dfrac{2}{9} =$

23) $\dfrac{8}{9} - \dfrac{5}{9} =$

24) $\dfrac{8}{10} - \dfrac{3}{10} =$

1) $\dfrac{4}{6} - \dfrac{6}{10} =$

2) $\dfrac{5}{8} - \dfrac{5}{10} =$

3) $\dfrac{8}{9} - \dfrac{6}{9} =$

4) $\dfrac{4}{5} - \dfrac{7}{9} =$

5) $\dfrac{7}{10} - \dfrac{1}{3} =$

6) $\dfrac{6}{10} - \dfrac{1}{10} =$

7) $\dfrac{4}{9} - \dfrac{2}{7} =$

8) $\dfrac{4}{7} - \dfrac{2}{4} =$

9) $\dfrac{8}{10} - \dfrac{8}{10} =$

10) $\dfrac{1}{6} - \dfrac{1}{9} =$

11) $\dfrac{5}{7} - \dfrac{3}{10} =$

12) $\dfrac{2}{4} - \dfrac{1}{4} =$

13) $\dfrac{4}{6} - \dfrac{1}{6} =$

14) $\dfrac{2}{4} - \dfrac{1}{10} =$

15) $\dfrac{5}{9} - \dfrac{3}{7} =$

16) $\dfrac{4}{6} - \dfrac{2}{6} =$

17) $\dfrac{8}{10} - \dfrac{1}{2} =$

18) $\dfrac{8}{9} - \dfrac{5}{9} =$

19) $\dfrac{4}{5} - \dfrac{1}{7} =$

20) $\dfrac{9}{10} - \dfrac{1}{9} =$

21) $\dfrac{9}{10} - \dfrac{2}{6} =$

22) $\dfrac{3}{9} - \dfrac{1}{9} =$

23) $\dfrac{6}{8} - \dfrac{2}{9} =$

24) $\dfrac{8}{9} - \dfrac{2}{10} =$

1) $\dfrac{4}{5} - \dfrac{4}{7} =$

2) $\dfrac{7}{8} - \dfrac{1}{8} =$

3) $\dfrac{5}{7} - \dfrac{2}{5} =$

4) $\dfrac{4}{10} - \dfrac{3}{9} =$

5) $\dfrac{2}{8} - \dfrac{1}{8} =$

6) $\dfrac{4}{10} - \dfrac{1}{6} =$

7) $\dfrac{4}{5} - \dfrac{4}{5} =$

8) $\dfrac{5}{10} - \dfrac{4}{10} =$

9) $\dfrac{4}{8} - \dfrac{2}{6} =$

10) $\dfrac{5}{7} - \dfrac{6}{10} =$

11) $\dfrac{4}{9} - \dfrac{3}{10} =$

12) $\dfrac{5}{10} - \dfrac{3}{6} =$

13) $\dfrac{7}{8} - \dfrac{7}{8} =$

14) $\dfrac{9}{10} - \dfrac{7}{10} =$

15) $\dfrac{8}{10} - \dfrac{4}{8} =$

16) $\dfrac{3}{4} - \dfrac{4}{9} =$

17) $\dfrac{1}{2} - \dfrac{4}{10} =$

18) $\dfrac{2}{5} - \dfrac{1}{7} =$

19) $\dfrac{4}{8} - \dfrac{1}{9} =$

20) $\dfrac{7}{8} - \dfrac{5}{10} =$

21) $\dfrac{3}{6} - \dfrac{3}{6} =$

22) $\dfrac{6}{7} - \dfrac{1}{6} =$

23) $\dfrac{3}{5} - \dfrac{1}{8} =$

24) $\dfrac{3}{4} - \dfrac{3}{4} =$

1) $7 \dfrac{2}{10} - \dfrac{2}{10} =$

2) $7 \dfrac{6}{8} - \dfrac{4}{7} =$

3) $\dfrac{8}{10} - \dfrac{4}{10} =$

4) $9 \dfrac{8}{9} - \dfrac{6}{7} =$

5) $9 \dfrac{4}{10} - \dfrac{2}{10} =$

6) $10 \dfrac{3}{6} - \dfrac{1}{6}$

7) $9 \dfrac{8}{9} - \dfrac{2}{9} =$

8) $4 \dfrac{9}{10} - \dfrac{4}{10} =$

9) $5 \dfrac{6}{9} - \dfrac{7}{8} =$

10) $8 \dfrac{5}{8} - \dfrac{2}{6} =$

11) $5 \dfrac{8}{9} - \dfrac{7}{9} =$

12) $7 \dfrac{4}{9} - \dfrac{1}{5} =$

13) $\dfrac{1}{2} - \dfrac{1}{9} =$

14) $8 \dfrac{4}{7} - \dfrac{1}{7} =$

15) $\dfrac{2}{3} - \dfrac{6}{9} =$

16) $5 \dfrac{1}{3} - \dfrac{2}{7} =$

1) $10 \frac{4}{8} - \frac{4}{7} =$

2) $7 \frac{7}{8} - \frac{2}{8} =$

3) $9 \frac{1}{3} - \frac{1}{6} =$

4) $8 \frac{1}{10} - \frac{8}{10} =$

5) $8 \frac{4}{10} - \frac{2}{3} =$

6) $9 \frac{3}{9} - \frac{9}{10} =$

7) $9 \frac{2}{9} - \frac{8}{9} =$

8) $8 \frac{1}{10} - \frac{1}{9} =$

9) $\frac{5}{7} - \frac{3}{8} =$

10) $6 \frac{2}{9} - \frac{4}{9} =$

11) $9 \frac{9}{10} - \frac{5}{9} =$

12) $8 \frac{6}{8} - \frac{3}{6} =$

13) $4 \frac{4}{9} - \frac{2}{8} =$

14) $9 \frac{4}{10} - \frac{1}{10} =$

15) $10 \frac{2}{6} - \frac{2}{7} =$

16) $8 \frac{8}{9} - \frac{6}{10} =$

TIME:

DATE:

SCORE:
/

1) $9\frac{3}{7} - \frac{4}{9} =$

2) $9\frac{5}{8} - \frac{3}{6} =$

3) $8\frac{4}{5} - \frac{1}{5} =$

4) $7\frac{6}{9} - \frac{7}{9} =$

5) $10\frac{9}{10} - \frac{5}{9} =$

6) $\frac{5}{6} - \frac{4}{9} =$

7) $6\frac{7}{9} - \frac{1}{9} =$

8) $\frac{4}{5} - \frac{3}{7} =$

9) $8\frac{7}{10} - \frac{1}{5} =$

10) $6\frac{7}{10} - \frac{8}{9} =$

11) $9\frac{7}{10} - \frac{8}{10} =$

12) $7\frac{4}{5} - \frac{3}{10} =$

13) $8\frac{7}{9} - \frac{4}{7} =$

14) $5\frac{4}{7} - \frac{4}{7} =$

15) $7\frac{5}{6} - \frac{4}{6} =$

16) $10\frac{1}{7} - \frac{2}{3}$

1.0
(A) 100000 %
(B) 10000 %
(C) 1 %
(D) 100 %

0.9
(A) 900 %
(B) 9 %
(C) 9000 %
(D) 90 %

1.7
(A) 170 %
(B) 170000 %
(C) 17 %
(D) 1.7 %

1.9
(A) 19 %
(B) 19000 %
(C) 190 %
(D) 1.9 %

1.4
(A) 14 %
(B) 1400 %
(C) 140 %
(D) 14000 %

1.6
(A) 16000 %
(B) 1.6 %
(C) 0.16 %
(D) 160 %

2.0
(A) 2 %
(B) 200000 %
(C) 200 %
(D) 0.2 %

1.2
(A) 120 %
(B) 1200 %
(C) 1.2 %
(D) 12 %

0.6
(A) 60 %
(B) 600 %
(C) 6000 %
(D) 0.06 %

0.7
(A) 70 %
(B) 70000 %
(C) 0.7 %
(D) 7 %

0.3
(A) 30 %
(B) 30000 %
(C) 0.3 %
(D) 3000 %

1.3
(A) 1.3 %
(B) 130 %
(C) 1300 %
(D) 0.13 %

1.2
(A) 12 %
(B) 12000 %
(C) 0.12 %
(D) 120 %

0.7
(A) 70 %
(B) 7 %
(C) 7000 %
(D) 700 %

0.3
(A) 3 %
(B) 30 %
(C) 3000 %
(D) 30000 %

1.7
(A) 1.7 %
(B) 1700 %
(C) 170 %
(D) 0.17 %

0.9
(A) 90 %
(B) 900 %
(C) 0.9 %
(D) 90000 %

1.2
(A) 120000 %
(B) 1200 %
(C) 120 %
(D) 0.12 %

1.7
(A) 170 %
(B) 1.7 %
(C) 170000 %
(D) 17000 %

0.4
(A) 40 %
(B) 4 %
(C) 0.4 %
(D) 400 %

1.9
(A) 1900 %
(B) 19 %
(C) 19000 %
(D) 190 %

0.5
(A) 5 %
(B) 50 %
(C) 500 %
(D) 0.5 %

2.0
(A) 200000 %
(B) 2000 %
(C) 2 %
(D) 200 %

0.2
(A) 20 %
(B) 200 %
(C) 2000 %
(D) 20000 %

1.4
(A) 14000 %
(B) 0.14 %
(C) 1400 %
(D) 140 %

0.7
(A) 0.7 %
(B) 700 %
(C) 0.07 %
(D) 70 %

1.5
(A) 15000 %
(B) 1.5 %
(C) 150 %
(D) 15 %

1.3
(A) 130 %
(B) 0.13 %
(C) 1300 %
(D) 1.3 %

1.0
(A) 100 %
(B) 1000 %
(C) 0.1 %
(D) 10 %

0.8
(A) 800 %
(B) 8000 %
(C) 80 %
(D) 80000 %

0.8
(A) 80 %
(B) 0.8 %
(C) 800 %
(D) 8 %

0.9
(A) 90000 %
(B) 0.9 %
(C) 900 %
(D) 90 %

1.5
(A) 150 %
(B) 150000 %
(C) 0.15 %
(D) 15 %

1.6
(A) 0.16 %
(B) 160000 %
(C) 1600 %
(D) 160 %

0.2
(A) 20 %
(B) 200 %
(C) 0.02 %
(D) 2000 %

1.4
(A) 1400 %
(B) 140 %
(C) 140000 %
(D) 14000 %

0.4
(A) 4 %
(B) 40 %
(C) 40000 %
(D) 4000 %

0.8
(A) 800 %
(B) 8 %
(C) 0.08 %
(D) 80 %

0.9
(A) 0.09 %
(B) 90000 %
(C) 90 %
(D) 900 %

0.7
(A) 0.7 %
(B) 700 %
(C) 70 %
(D) 7 %

Model Answer

Page 4, Item 1:

(1)1198 (2)1155 (3)1342 (4)1622 (5)1117
(6)593 (7)981 (8)735 (9)1258 (10)666
(11)826 (12)1116 (13)1965 (14)1329
(15)552 (16)985 (17)1276 (18)1276 (19)712
(20)743 (21)841 (22)1127 (23)1008
(24)1083 (25)811 (26)675 (27)982 (28)1085
(29)737 (30)843 (31)927 (32)1739 (33)923
(34)1249 (35)1394 (36)682 (37)1845
(38)954 (39)458 (40)529

Page 5, Item 1:

(1)1376 (2)1301 (3)971 (4)984 (5)1004
(6)1039 (7)1038 (8)689 (9)415 (10)742
(11)1365 (12)892 (13)390 (14)1080
(15)1182 (16)1507 (17)1414 (18)1166
(19)606 (20)1156 (21)805 (22)642 (23)1294
(24)1113 (25)1236 (26)1315 (27)1612
(28)1364 (29)1428 (30)548 (31)640
(32)1329 (33)616 (34)744 (35)645 (36)592
(37)1555 (38)1196 (39)917 (40)1423

Page 6, Item 1:

(1)876 (2)661 (3)757 (4)793 (5)503 (6)640
(7)784 (8)290 (9)645 (10)471 (11)202
(12)366 (13)670 (14)810 (15)117 (16)437
(17)358 (18)493 (19)945 (20)656 (21)633
(22)801 (23)452 (24)519 (25)786 (26)263
(27)405 (28)838 (29)295 (30)906 (31)205
(32)951 (33)481 (34)188 (35)713 (36)568
(37)515 (38)863 (39)583 (40)961

Page 7, Item 1:

(1)562 (2)358 (3)990 (4)341 (5)524 (6)547
(7)185 (8)406 (9)999 (10)336 (11)504
(12)873 (13)716 (14)585 (15)976 (16)604
(17)597 (18)543 (19)585 (20)554 (21)270
(22)529 (23)341 (24)746 (25)667 (26)722
(27)814 (28)564 (29)287 (30)899 (31)447
(32)572 (33)270 (34)992 (35)409 (36)350
(37)130 (38)243 (39)915 (40)425

Page 8, Item 1:

(1)135 (2)647 (3)360 (4)809 (5)507 (6)692
(7)836 (8)466 (9)289 (10)584 (11)501
(12)776 (13)628 (14)351 (15)895 (16)616
(17)479 (18)467 (19)853 (20)660 (21)177
(22)686 (23)819 (24)922 (25)341 (26)305
(27)848 (28)905 (29)306 (30)366 (31)644
(32)489 (33)458 (34)613 (35)519 (36)796
(37)186 (38)530 (39)921 (40)921

Page 9, Item 1:

(1)1054 (2)1595 (3)1000 (4)774 (5)628
(6)1234 (7)829 (8)1817 (9)1390 (10)1194
(11)1642 (12)1412 (13)1564 (14)1017
(15)1123 (16)1087 (17)699 (18)790
(19)1124 (20)1386 (21)1302 (22)1722
(23)1063 (24)1157 (25)1093 (26)1468
(27)642 (28)693 (29)992 (30)1672 (31)1175
(32)1719 (33)1224 (34)887 (35)1638
(36)1265 (37)571 (38)1005 (39)671 (40)711

Page 10, Item 1:

(1)493 (2)167 (3)817 (4)535 (5)960 (6)527
(7)155 (8)819 (9)355 (10)640 (11)380
(12)940 (13)535 (14)854 (15)122 (16)829
(17)165 (18)975 (19)560 (20)996 (21)313
(22)809 (23)100 (24)621 (25)203 (26)947
(27)559 (28)975 (29)433 (30)207 (31)713
(32)330 (33)996 (34)125 (35)220 (36)908
(37)169 (38)615 (39)313 (40)857

Page 11, Item 1:

(1)713 (2)765 (3)950 (4)196 (5)186 (6)357
(7)615 (8)602 (9)380 (10)495 (11)262

(12)482 (13)457 (14)454 (15)233 (16)101
(17)276 (18)167 (19)961 (20)912 (21)660
(22)871 (23)982 (24)664 (25)964 (26)390
(27)328 (28)862 (29)568 (30)683 (31)873
(32)310 (33)408 (34)331 (35)756 (36)151
(37)564 (38)561 (39)424 (40)930

Page 12, Item 1:
(1)623 (2)79 (3)500 (4)486 (5)5 (6)0 (7)469
(8)558 (9)274 (10)660 (11)455 (12)456
(13)287 (14)141 (15)650 (16)408 (17)398
(18)522 (19)1 (20)83 (21)489 (22)51
(23)557 (24)774 (25)401 (26)194 (27)33
(28)289 (29)85 (30)64 (31)468 (32)711
(33)154 (34)466 (35)57 (36)391 (37)128
(38)358 (39)157 (40)287

Page 13, Item 1:
(1)140 (2)27 (3)459 (4)448 (5)35 (6)233
(7)354 (8)666 (9)152 (10)95 (11)668
(12)525 (13)284 (14)473 (15)287 (16)208
(17)399 (18)155 (19)86 (20)64 (21)617
(22)242 (23)101 (24)342 (25)14 (26)699
(27)87 (28)130 (29)432 (30)60 (31)746
(32)541 (33)333 (34)133 (35)494 (36)102
(37)71 (38)382 (39)84 (40)356

Page 14, Item 1:
(1)910 (2)223 (3)733 (4)395 (5)900 (6)580
(7)397 (8)889 (9)689 (10)862 (11)306
(12)744 (13)713 (14)804 (15)775 (16)885
(17)646 (18)700 (19)317 (20)898 (21)949
(22)776 (23)903 (24)904 (25)576 (26)718
(27)495 (28)913 (29)614 (30)921 (31)808
(32)922 (33)724 (34)598 (35)856 (36)808
(37)453 (38)763 (39)967 (40)235

Page 15, Item 1:
(1)338 (2)210 (3)402 (4)440 (5)186 (6)244
(7)515 (8)90 (9)328 (10)93 (11)351 (12)293
(13)629 (14)421 (15)396 (16)110 (17)341
(18)122 (19)119 (20)217 (21)355 (22)256
(23)33 (24)302 (25)184 (26)438 (27)160

(28)63 (29)667 (30)873 (31)88 (32)93
(33)252 (34)257 (35)246 (36)416 (37)32
(38)279 (39)262 (40)410

Page 16, Item 1:
(1)538 (2)539 (3)665 (4)798 (5)295 (6)517
(7)770 (8)975 (9)763 (10)392 (11)840
(12)778 (13)906 (14)579 (15)977 (16)618
(17)771 (18)887 (19)332 (20)606 (21)940
(22)340 (23)860 (24)911 (25)736 (26)926
(27)590 (28)598 (29)872 (30)920 (31)359
(32)727 (33)559 (34)995 (35)547 (36)722
(37)865 (38)661 (39)843 (40)861

Page 17, Item 1:
(1)583 (2)625 (3)600 (4)529 (5)288 (6)306
(7)342 (8)164 (9)669 (10)157 (11)294
(12)402 (13)365 (14)453 (15)530 (16)194
(17)409 (18)606 (19)335 (20)565 (21)292
(22)765 (23)309 (24)529 (25)313 (26)673
(27)367 (28)340 (29)940 (30)102 (31)361
(32)448 (33)525 (34)365 (35)155 (36)615
(37)837 (38)616 (39)421 (40)250

Page 18, Item 1:
(1)523 (2)448 (3)416 (4)213 (5)178 (6)107
(7)100 (8)623 (9)673 (10)424 (11)580
(12)238 (13)309 (14)672 (15)514 (16)327
(17)854 (18)652 (19)250 (20)387 (21)252
(22)416 (23)148 (24)202 (25)232 (26)130
(27)667 (28)184 (29)491 (30)116 (31)146

(32)165 (33)426 (34)349 (35)333 (36)444
(37)374 (38)367 (39)904 (40)284

Page 19, Item 1:
(1)129 (2)158 (3)65 (4)91 (5)539 (6)369
(7)41 (8)57 (9)207 (10)58 (11)429 (12)271
(13)664 (14)144 (15)37 (16)182 (17)424
(18)512 (19)478 (20)109 (21)167 (22)71
(23)441 (24)247 (25)433 (26)64 (27)386
(28)555 (29)388 (30)359 (31)426 (32)89
(33)288 (34)774 (35)37 (36)147 (37)125
(38)218 (39)307 (40)463

Page 20, Item 1:
(1)28 (2)56 (3)27 (4)45 (5)20 (6)7 (7)1 (8)36
(9)2 (10)16 (11)49 (12)18 (13)3 (14)21
(15)81 (16)4 (17)20 (18)5 (19)24 (20)5
(21)6 (22)16 (23)30 (24)40 (25)27 (26)8
(27)4 (28)30 (29)9 (30)7 (31)6 (32)27
(33)24 (34)18 (35)7 (36)8 (37)63 (38)36
(39)8 (40)21

Page 21, Item 1:
(1)9 (2)12 (3)64 (4)81 (5)63 (6)21 (7)6 (8)30
(9)18 (10)4 (11)5 (12)25 (13)12 (14)18
(15)45 (16)32 (17)42 (18)12 (19)5 (20)4
(21)8 (22)54 (23)16 (24)36 (25)56 (26)7
(27)30 (28)35 (29)4 (30)8 (31)24 (32)10
(33)40 (34)10 (35)48 (36)14 (37)81 (38)3
(39)40 (40)24

Page 22, Item 1:
(1)21 (2)5 (3)20 (4)5 (5)8 (6)21 (7)12 (8)30
(9)40 (10)63 (11)2 (12)30 (13)24 (14)8
(15)49 (16)36 (17)21 (18)15 (19)7 (20)36
(21)45 (22)48 (23)12 (24)32 (25)2 (26)5
(27)3 (28)24 (29)35 (30)36 (31)56 (32)8
(33)21 (34)12 (35)48 (36)36 (37)30 (38)20
(39)36 (40)36

Page 23, Item 1:
(1)35 (2)24 (3)9 (4)6 (5)3 (6)10 (7)18 (8)24
(9)3 (10)4 (11)24 (12)10 (13)20 (14)9 (15)5
(16)16 (17)27 (18)63 (19)30 (20)15 (21)45

(22)45 (23)12 (24)4 (25)10 (26)4 (27)18
(28)8 (29)7 (30)9 (31)64 (32)12 (33)21
(34)8 (35)24 (36)2 (37)63 (38)5 (39)6 (40)8

Page 24, Item 1:
(1)6 (2)5 (3)4 (4)8 (5)2 (6)1 (7)7 (8)8 (9)8
(10)1 (11)6 (12)8 (13)2 (14)2 (15)8 (16)5
(17)2 (18)5 (19)2 (20)9 (21)6 (22)5 (23)7
(24)7 (25)6 (26)2 (27)7 (28)6 (29)5 (30)2
(31)6 (32)8 (33)3 (34)1 (35)9 (36)2 (37)4
(38)4 (39)7 (40)4

Page 25, Item 1:
(1)9 (2)7 (3)3 (4)2 (5)3 (6)2 (7)4 (8)5 (9)2
(10)9 (11)3 (12)9 (13)3 (14)1 (15)7 (16)7
(17)8 (18)8 (19)9 (20)2 (21)4 (22)2 (23)8
(24)5 (25)2 (26)2 (27)9 (28)8 (29)5 (30)7
(31)9 (32)6 (33)5 (34)6 (35)9 (36)5 (37)5
(38)7 (39)6 (40)9

Page 26, Item 1:
(1)2 (2)6 (3)7 (4)1 (5)4 (6)3 (7)4 (8)5 (9)1
(10)2 (11)9 (12)7 (13)3 (14)8 (15)7 (16)8
(17)8 (18)3 (19)7 (20)7 (21)8 (22)4 (23)6
(24)4 (25)4 (26)7 (27)6 (28)8 (29)7 (30)1
(31)9 (32)1 (33)4 (34)4 (35)8 (36)8 (37)3
(38)2 (39)7 (40)6

Page 27, Item 1:
(1)1 (2)6 (3)2 (4)8 (5)8 (6)7 (7)7 (8)3 (9)5
(10)8 (11)2 (12)8 (13)5 (14)3 (15)3 (16)8
(17)5 (18)7 (19)1 (20)6 (21)1 (22)5 (23)2
(24)2 (25)8 (26)5 (27)7 (28)7 (29)7 (30)5
(31)8 (32)5 (33)6 (34)5 (35)5 (36)5 (37)6
(38)3 (39)7 (40)3

Page 28, Item 1:
(1)7 (2)2 (3)5 (4)6 (5)9 (6)8 (7)9 (8)9 (9)9
(10)6 (11)4 (12)2 (13)8 (14)6 (15)6 (16)1
(17)6 (18)1 (19)4 (20)4 (21)3 (22)5 (23)2
(24)9 (25)6 (26)7 (27)7 (28)5 (29)5 (30)9
(31)9 (32)6 (33)7 (34)2 (35)6 (36)3 (37)6
(38)5 (39)5 (40)8

Page 29, Item 1:
(1)2 (2)3 (3)8 (4)7 (5)3 (6)4 (7)1 (8)7 (9)8
(10)5 (11)5 (12)4 (13)4 (14)6 (15)9 (16)5
(17)2 (18)4 (19)3 (20)3 (21)4 (22)6 (23)7
(24)9 (25)4 (26)5 (27)2 (28)2 (29)4 (30)3
(31)2 (32)2 (33)9 (34)3 (35)6 (36)3 (37)4
(38)3 (39)5 (40)8

Page 30, Item 1:
(1)7 (2)19 (3)9 (4)2 (5)6 (6)46 (7)25 (8)13
(9)16 (10)2 (11)4 (12)16 (13)28 (14)26
(15)7 (16)9 (17)28 (18)5 (19)13 (20)2 (21)5
(22)29 (23)28 (24)8 (25)24 (26)29 (27)9
(28)26 (29)3 (30)16 (31)6 (32)27 (33)4
(34)3 (35)4 (36)5 (37)15 (38)15 (39)35
(40)29

Page 31, Item 1:
(1)7 (2)79 (3)82 (4)3 (5)65 (6)1 (7)19 (8)10
(9)81 (10)7 (11)19 (12)86 (13)56 (14)13
(15)84 (16)3 (17)7 (18)4 (19)89 (20)14
(21)11 (22)70 (23)49 (24)8 (25)2 (26)67
(27)43 (28)41 (29)1 (30)72 (31)16 (32)23
(33)12 (34)13 (35)39 (36)6 (37)73 (38)61
(39)38 (40)73

Page 32, Item 1:
(1)97 (2)1 (3)73 (4)46 (5)14 (6)8 (7)29 (8)53
(9)47 (10)25 (11)7 (12)57 (13)78 (14)13
(15)9 (16)22 (17)2 (18)16 (19)13 (20)1
(21)20 (22)16 (23)91 (24)24 (25)37 (26)44
(27)30 (28)37 (29)53 (30)39 (31)53 (32)3
(33)49 (34)18 (35)3 (36)22 (37)10 (38)71
(39)39 (40)85

Page 33, Item 1:
(1)17 (2)3 (3)29 (4)89 (5)7 (6)25 (7)27 (8)42
(9)90 (10)56 (11)9 (12)19 (13)15 (14)17
(15)35 (16)61 (17)38 (18)24 (19)4 (20)7
(21)26 (22)37 (23)60 (24)7 (25)57 (26)13
(27)38 (28)86 (29)48 (30)7 (31)49 (32)5
(33)97 (34)10 (35)8 (36)64 (37)42 (38)100
(39)20 (40)38

Page 34, Item 1:
(1)37 (2)81 (3)54 (4)21 (5)81 (6)14 (7)14
(8)54 (9)35 (10)7 (11)29 (12)25 (13)11
(14)94 (15)63 (16)81 (17)42 (18)54 (19)99
(20)59 (21)65 (22)75 (23)81 (24)73 (25)94
(26)9 (27)35 (28)40 (29)14 (30)76 (31)65
(32)52 (33)38 (34)73 (35)82 (36)52 (37)96
(38)12 (39)50 (40)49

Page 35, Item 1:
(1)58 (2)98 (3)4 (4)74 (5)72 (6)48 (7)49 (8)1
(9)69 (10)96 (11)74 (12)85 (13)62 (14)30
(15)78 (16)82 (17)11 (18)69 (19)2 (20)43
(21)34 (22)14 (23)50 (24)50 (25)55 (26)52
(27)23 (28)32 (29)40 (30)20 (31)77 (32)4
(33)79 (34)57 (35)28 (36)40 (37)31 (38)9
(39)73 (40)65

Page 36, Item 1:
(1)8 (2)2 (3)1 (4)1 (5)1 (6)6 (7)1 (8)1 (9)2
(10)1 (11)9 (12)1 (13)1 (14)2 (15)2 (16)1
(17)2 (18)1 (19)1 (20)1 (21)2 (22)2 (23)3
(24)1 (25)2 (26)4 (27)1 (28)1 (29)1 (30)6
(31)1 (32)4 (33)1 (34)1 (35)2 (36)2 (37)1
(38)2 (39)2 (40)3

Page 37, Item 1:
(1)3 (2)1 (3)1 (4)3 (5)1 (6)1 (7)3 (8)3 (9)3
(10)8 (11)4 (12)6 (13)3 (14)2 (15)7 (16)3
(17)1 (18)1 (19)5 (20)9 (21)2 (22)8 (23)1
(24)1 (25)4 (26)3 (27)2 (28)6 (29)3 (30)8
(31)2 (32)1 (33)1 (34)2 (35)3 (36)1 (37)1
(38)7 (39)3 (40)1

Page 38, Item 1:
(1)4 (2)7 (3)3 (4)3 (5)3 (6)5 (7)1 (8)3 (9)4
(10)6 (11)1 (12)1 (13)1 (14)1 (15)7 (16)3
(17)1 (18)2 (19)1 (20)3 (21)1 (22)2 (23)1
(24)1 (25)1 (26)2 (27)3 (28)1 (29)1 (30)1
(31)4 (32)1 (33)1 (34)3 (35)1 (36)1 (37)2
(38)3 (39)1 (40)2

Page 39, Item 1:

(1)
```
      2 5
  1 ) 2 5
    - 2
      0 5
    -   5
        0
```
(2)
```
      3 7
  2 ) 7 4
    - 6
      1 4
    - 1 4
        0
```
(3)
```
          3
  5 ) 1 5
    - 1 5
        0
```
(4)
```
          3
  5 ) 1 5
    - 1 5
        0
```
(5)
```
      1 8
  1 ) 1 8
    - 1
      0 8
    -   8
        0
```
(6)
```
      1 2
  8 ) 9 6
    - 8
      1 6
    - 1 6
        0
```

Page 40, Item 1:

(1)
```
      1 7
  5 ) 8 5
    - 5
      3 5
    - 3 5
        0
```
(2)
```
      3 7
  2 ) 7 4
    - 6
      1 4
    - 1 4
        0
```
(3)
```
      2 5
  2 ) 5 0
    - 4
      1 0
    - 1 0
        0
```
(4)
```
      2 5
  2 ) 5 0
    - 4
      1 0
    - 1 0
        0
```
(5)
```
      3 8
  2 ) 7 6
    - 6
      1 6
    - 1 6
        0
```
(6)
```
          6
  3 ) 1 8
    - 1 8
        0
```

Page 41, Item 1:
(1)6:00 (2)7:00 (3)7:00 (4)11:00 (5)10:00
(6)9:00 (7)11:00 (8)1:00 (9)7:00

Page 42, Item 1:
(1)5:00 (2)8:00 (3)2:00 (4)7:00 (5)5:00
(6)3:00 (7)5:00 (8)3:00 (9)6:00

Page 43, Item 1:
(1)6 (2)5 (3)4 (4)11 (5)10 (6)7 (7)3 (8)5 (9)4

Page 44, Item 1:

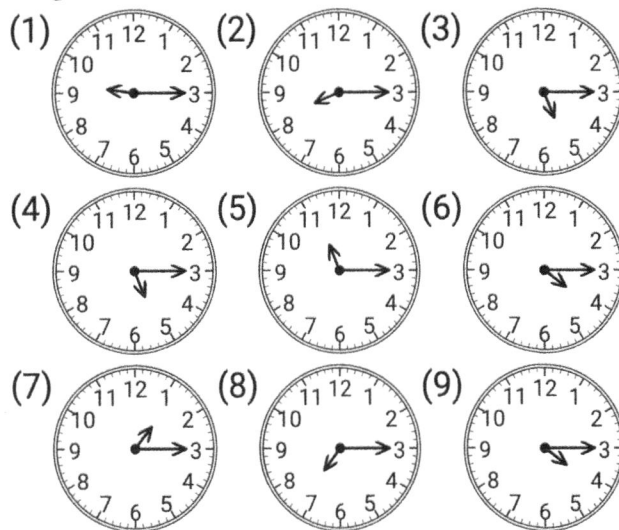

69

Page 45, Item 1:

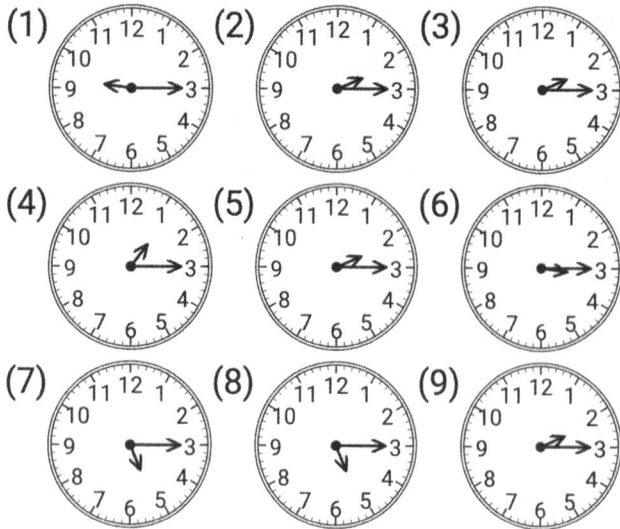

(1) (2) (3)
(4) (5) (6)
(7) (8) (9)

Page 46, Item 1:
(1)5/9 (2)6/5 (3)7/8 (4)13/10 (5)11/7 (6)4/8
(7)6/7 (8)9/9 (9)2/9 (10)7/8 (11)10/9
(12)11/8 (13)6/8 (14)7/9 (15)7/6 (16)13/9
(17)5/8 (18)11/9 (19)9/7 (20)14/10
(21)11/8 (22)3/4 (23)11/8 (24)9/9

Page 47, Item 1:
(1)6/7 (2)13/10 (3)2/4 (4)5/7 (5)2/9 (6)4/4
(7)7/7 (8)5/10 (9)8/7 (10)6/6 (11)4/4
(12)9/9 (13)5/5 (14)9/8 (15)7/10 (16)6/5
(17)3/4 (18)12/10 (19)13/9 (20)8/8
(21)10/9 (22)8/8 (23)3/3 (24)12/10

Page 48, Item 1:
(1)10/9 (2)10/21 (3)16/24 (4)86/70
(5)55/50 (6)4/7 (7)112/80 (8)93/72 (9)5/6
(10)44/32 (11)5/8 (12)54/70 (13)14/10
(14)42/40 (15)54/54 (16)72/54 (17)20/32
(18)3/7 (19)91/90 (20)25/21 (21)5/8
(22)5/8 (23)34/80 (24)62/40

Page 49, Item 1:
(1)20/42 (2)7/6 (3)51/56 (4)6/7 (5)74/72
(6)33/27 (7)11/10 (8)54/40 (9)93/54
(10)9/9 (11)36/35 (12)49/72 (13)10/10
(14)34/36 (15)14/48 (16)8/8 (17)54/40
(18)85/70 (19)15/9 (20)18/28 (21)9/10
(22)67/72 (23)30/28 (24)3/4

Page 50, Item 1:
(1)8/4 (2)113/72 (3)146/70 (4)15/9 (5)45/8
(6)16/3 (7)99/30 (8)108/48 (9)8/9
(10)38/28 (11)50/24 (12)12/8 (13)22/35
(14)12/10 (15)9/9 (16)9/10 (17)53/8
(18)164/80 (19)16/7 (20)39/9 (21)49/24
(22)7/6 (23)47/35 (24)108/80

Page 51, Item 1:
(1)7/5 (2)42/48 (3)11/4 (4)5/3 (5)39/20
(6)117/90 (7)81/56 (8)12/6 (9)132/90
(10)60/9 (11)110/45 (12)11/4 (13)11/15
(14)4/4 (15)68/28 (16)6/10 (17)10/9
(18)52/72 (19)76/45 (20)145/90 (21)11/3
(22)4/3 (23)66/28 (24)7/10

Page 52, Item 1:
(1)6/7 (2)98/36 (3)52/60 (4)18/27 (5)81/42
(6)6/6 (7)46/48 (8)40/40 (9)16/9
(10)150/80 (11)9/7 (12)33/54 (13)50/56
(14)57/72 (15)4/8 (16)10/3 (17)45/50
(18)41/36 (19)26/12 (20)92/70 (21)7/5
(22)77/45 (23)6/10 (24)9/4

Page 53, Item 1:
(1)89/6 (2)105/10 (3)76/8 (4)111/8
(5)132/8 (6)107/9 (7)108/9 (8)107/8
(9)99/7 (10)131/10 (11)157/9 (12)30/3
(13)111/7 (14)73/8 (15)105/9 (16)81/7

Page 54, Item 1:
(1)87/9 (2)102/6 (3)136/7 (4)57/7 (5)39/6
(6)141/8 (7)65/10 (8)120/6 (9)143/8
(10)156/9 (11)84/6 (12)33/7 (13)144/9
(14)39/3 (15)27/5 (16)62/7

Page 55, Item 1:
(1)3/6 (2)0/5 (3)2/9 (4)0/5 (5)0/10 (6)3/7
(7)5/10 (8)1/6 (9)0/9 (10)0/10 (11)2/9
(12)5/10 (13)4/10 (14)4/10 (15)4/8 (16)2/9
(17)1/10 (18)0/8 (19)3/10 (20)0/10 (21)0/6
(22)3/8 (23)0/9 (24)0/8

Page 56, Item 1:
(1)0/4 (2)6/10 (3)3/9 (4)1/5 (5)0/7 (6)0/5
(7)1/10 (8)1/7 (9)1/6 (10)0/3 (11)2/9
(12)0/9 (13)3/10 (14)0/8 (15)5/9 (16)3/9
(17)1/10 (18)1/9 (19)1/6 (20)1/10 (21)2/7
(22)4/9 (23)3/9 (24)5/10

Page 57, Item 1:
(1)4/60 (2)10/80 (3)2/9 (4)1/45 (5)11/30
(6)5/10 (7)10/63 (8)2/28 (9)0/10 (10)3/54
(11)29/70 (12)1/4 (13)3/6 (14)16/40
(15)8/63 (16)2/6 (17)6/20 (18)3/9
(19)23/35 (20)71/90 (21)34/60 (22)2/9
(23)38/72 (24)62/90

Page 58, Item 1:
(1)8/35 (2)6/8 (3)11/35 (4)6/90 (5)1/8
(6)14/60 (7)0/5 (8)1/10 (9)8/48 (10)8/70
(11)13/90 (12)0/60 (13)0/8 (14)2/10
(15)24/80 (16)11/36 (17)2/20 (18)9/35
(19)28/72 (20)30/80 (21)0/6 (22)29/42
(23)19/40 (24)0/4

Page 59, Item 1:
(1)70/10 (2)402/56 (3)4/10 (4)569/63
(5)92/10 (6)62/6 (7)87/9 (8)45/10
(9)345/72 (10)398/48 (11)46/9 (12)326/45
(13)7/18 (14)59/7 (15)0/27 (16)106/21

Page 60, Item 1:
(1)556/56 (2)61/8 (3)165/18 (4)73/10
(5)232/30 (6)759/90 (7)75/9 (8)719/90
(9)19/56 (10)52/9 (11)841/90 (12)396/48
(13)302/72 (14)93/10 (15)422/42
(16)746/90

Page 61, Item 1:
(1)566/63 (2)438/48 (3)43/5 (4)62/9

(5)931/90 (6)21/54 (7)60/9 (8)13/35
(9)425/50 (10)523/90 (11)89/10
(12)375/50 (13)517/63 (14)35/7 (15)43/6
(16)199/21

Page 62, Item 1:
(1)D (2)D (3)A (4)C (5)C (6)D (7)C (8)A (9)A
(10)A (11)A (12)B (13)D (14)A (15)B (16)C
(17)A (18)C (19)A (20)A

Page 63, Item 1:
(1)D (2)B (3)D (4)A (5)D (6)D (7)C (8)A (9)A
(10)C (11)A (12)D (13)A (14)D (15)A (16)B
(17)B (18)D (19)C (20)C

Made in the USA
Middletown, DE
05 September 2024